NO ORDER OF PRECEDENCE	Can Interrupt?	Requires Second?	Amendable	Debatable?	Vote Required?
INCIDENTAL MOTIONS					
POINT OF ORDER	Interrupts	⊘Second	⊘Amendable	⊘Debatable	No Vote
APPEAL	Interrupts	Second	⊘Amendable	Debatable	Majority
PARLIAMENTARY INQUIRY	Interrupts	⊘Second	⊘Amendable	⊘Debatable	No Vote
POINT OF INFORMATION	Interrupts	⊘Second	⊘Amendable	⊘Debatable	No Vote
DIVISION OF THE ASSEMBLY	Interrupts	⊘Second	⊘Amendable	⊘Debatable	No Vote
DIVISION OF A QUESTION	⊘Interrupts	Second	Amendable	⊘Debatable	Majority
SUSPEND THE RULES	⊘Interrupts	Second	⊘Amendable	⊘Debatable	2/3
RESTORATIVE MOTIONS					
RECONSIDER	Interrupts	Second	⊘Amendable	Debatable	Majority
RECIND OR AMEND SOMETHING PREVIOUSLY ADOPTED	⊘Interrupts	Second	Amendable	Debatable	2/3
TAKE FROM THE TABLE	⊘Interrupts	Second	⊘Amendable	⊘Debatable	Majority

The ⊘ symbol means "no." For example, ⊘Interrupts means
⊘Debatable mear

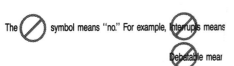

To the men and women
of the
Cincinnati Bible College & Seminary
Whose lives and ministries
reflect the Light of the World

© Copyright 1987 • Broadman Press

All rights reserved

4231-16

ISBN: 0-8054-3116-0

Dewey Decimal Classification: 060.4

Subject Heading: PARLIAMENTARY PRACTICE

Library of Congress Catalog Card Number: 87-6364

Library of Congress Cataloging-in-Publication Data

McCarty, C. Barry, 1953-
    A parliamentary guide for church leaders.

    Includes index.
    1. Church meetings.   2. Parliamentary practice.
I. Title.
BV652.15.M37   1987   254   87-6364
ISBN 0-8054-3116-0

Acknowledgments

My list of people to whom thanks is due for making possible the writing of this book begins with my mother, Lorraine Chesnut, my late father, Leroy McCarty, and my stepfather, Richard Chesnut, all of whose exemplary service in the Lord's kingdom has taught me the eternal significance of what churches do.

Much of what I have learned about parliamentary procedure I owe to three dear friends and fellow professional parliamentarians: Mr. Lester L. Dahms, Past President and Past Executive Director of the American Institute of Parliamentarians; Dr. M. Eugene Bierbaum, Past President of AIP and Professor of Speech at the State University of New York at Cortland; and Dr. Floyd M. Riddick, Parliamentarian Emeritus of the United States Senate and author of the first revision of the Senate's rules since Thomas Jefferson wrote the original manual.

Two other friends have made possible my participation in state and national political affairs: Senator Jesse Helms, himself a master of parliamentary strategy; and the Governor of North Carolina, Jim Martin, in whose administration I have had the opportunity to practice some of the finer points of the deliberative arts.

Special thanks is due Dr. Charles Stanley, Dr. Adrian Rogers, and Dr. Jerry Vines for the pleasure of assisting them in presiding over the world's largest deliberative assembly, the Southern Baptist Convention.

Finally, to my children, Ryan, Noah, and Ian, and their mother, Pat, thanks for being quiet so Daddy could finish his book.

Foreword

When you think of spiritual leadership, what qualities come to mind? No doubt high on your list are such attributes as vision, zeal, perseverance, and integrity.

While those are fundamental, they must all be administered and exercised in an ordered, disciplined manner or else chaos and confusion will reign.

During my tenure as president of the Southern Baptist Convention, I discovered the blunt reality of that truth. Though great plans to carry out God's glorious call of evangelism and edification were being formulated at all levels during the annual convention, the very mass of people involved in that process, almost 50,000 was overwhelming. How could we seek God's mind and at the same time acknowledge the often divergent viewpoints of the participants so that we could conclude with one mind and one accord?

Thankfully God's grace led me to Dr. C. Barry McCarty, a former professor of public speaking and debate, now president of Cincinnati Bible College & Seminary, and a Certified Professional Parliamentarian.

Through his personal involvement on the convention podium, we were able to proceed properly and harmoniously in accomplishing the mighty plans of God. I am indebted to him for his counsel and wisdom, both spiritual and vocational.

Thankfully, Dr. McCarty has now made his expertise available to godly leaders who seek to obey Paul's admonition that "all things be done decently and in order" (1 Cor. 14:40).

Whether your church or ministry is large or small, Dr. McCarty's precise and helpful manual is of enormous benefit. Following the principles established in the renowned *Roberts Rules of Orders Newly Revised,* Dr. McCarty presents workable guidelines for promoting biblical unity. It provides a streamlined form through which all parties may be duly recognized and through which agreements may be peaceably forged.

As spiritual leaders implement the tenets of this manual, they will earn the respect of those who follow, by doing not only what is right in the sight of God but also of men. The end result is that God's kingdom is effectively and fruitfully advanced.

Through the crucible of personal experience, I encourage all who are entrusted with spiritual leadership to eagerly digest Dr. McCarty's *A Parliamentary Guide for Church Leaders.* If you haven't needed its counsel before, I assure you the time will come.

When it does, you will have been prepared to cheerfully experience the fulfillment of Psalm 133:1-2: "Behold, how good and how pleasant it is for brethren to dwell together in unity! It is like the precious ointment upon the head, that ran down upon the beard, even Aaron's beard."

DR. CHARLES STANLEY

Contents

1
Introduction

In 1863 a U.S. Army officer who was active in his church was assigned to construct defenses for the port of New Bedford, Massachusetts. While there the gentleman was asked, without warning, to preside over a business meeting of his church. Though he was an officer in the Corps of Engineers and had participated in church and civic affairs wherever he was stationed, he did not know how to preside at a meeting. Embarrassed, but feeling the worst thing he could do would be to decline, he plunged into the meeting hoping that the assembly would behave itself. It did not. The officer emerged from that turbulent meeting determined that he would never again attend another until he knew something about parliamentary law.

Though various parliamentary manuals were available, the gentleman learned that there was no generally accepted set of parliamentary rules for voluntary associations, such as churches and civic groups. So, he set out to write one. That man was Henry M. Robert, author of *Robert's Rules of Order,* the famous manual that has dominated the field of parliamentary procedure for over a century.

I tell that story for two reasons. First, if you have picked up this book because you have been or will be put on the spot by having to preside or participate in a meeting and you are not sure exactly what to do, I wanted you to know that the man whose name is synonymous with parliamentary procedure was once in your shoes. Second, I wanted you to know that General Robert wrote his now familiar guide to help churches conduct their business more efficiently.

Then why can't church leaders and members simply pick up a copy of *Robert's Rules* and learn what they need to know to conduct their meetings? The problem is that Henry Robert's pocket manual has grown larger and more complex with each new edition. When first published in 1876, the book was a modest 176 pages long. The latest edition of *Robert's Rules of Order Newly Revised* runs over 600 pages.[1] The book's comprehensiveness happens to be one of its strengths. Anything about parliamentary procedure that is not in *Robert's Rules,* you probably do not need anyway. Still, to most novices the book appears as a tangled web of parliamentary technicalities.

The problem is not so much in the content or size of the book as in how it is used. Whatever it was in the beginning, *Robert's Rules of Order Newly Revised* is not a textbook, but a reference manual. As a codification of rules, it reads very much like a legal document. In a sense, that is precisely what it is. But trying to learn how to preside or participate in a meeting just by reading *Robert's Rules* is like trying to learn how to drive by reading your state's traffic code.

My purpose for writing this book is to give church leaders and members a simplified, unintimidating, practical guide to the rules and customs that govern deliberative assemblies. It is a book about how to get things done in a meeting. I have pared the parliamentary code down to the fundamental rules you must know to be able to propose, oppose, or dispose of a motion, to serve on a committee, to speak in debate, or to conduct a church business meeting. The book should also equip you to influence decisions made by your professional association, civic club, political party, local government, or any other organization in which you have an interest.

Once you have mastered the basics from this book, you should find *Robert's Rules* and other parliamentary codes less intimidating. You will have a basic framework in which to fit the advanced points of parliamentary procedure as you have need to learn them.

General Principles

Your study of specific rules can be easier from the start if you will first fix in your mind certain general principles on which the rules are based. Hundreds of rules and customs govern *deliberative assemblies*. Unless you are a professional parliamentarian, you do not need to learn them all. You will also occasionally find yourself in a parliamentary situation that the rules do not specifically address, but which would be covered by a general principle of parliamentary law. If you know these principles, you can figure out a lot of the rules.

1. Group Decisions Should Be Made in an Orderly Fashion.

Successful meetings are possible only when there is an orderly consideration of business. If an assembly had no rules to guide it, if each member could speak on any subject, as long and as many times as he pleased, if every member could speak at the same time, it would be impossible to reach a deliberate decision on any matter. The first object of parliamentary procedure, then, is to preserve order. The rules are aimed at providing an orderly forum in which an assembly can determine and express the will of its members on matters that come before them.

The two most fundamental rules of parliamentary procedure both have to do with preserving order. The first rule is that an assembly can consider only one thing at a time. When a subject is introduced by means of a *main motion,* that motion must be adopted, rejected, referred to a committee, postponed, or disposed of in some way before another subject can be introduced. Only one speaker may speak at a time, and he must confine his remarks to the immediately pending question. He cannot speak about anything other than the one subject before the group right then.

The second rule governs the use of the various kinds of motions. When any of the specialized motions are needed to help dispose of a main motion or to handle a procedural matter, these motions have a definite order of precedence, or rank, that determines when they can be introduced and considered.

The whole purpose of this system of motions and the one-thing-at-a-time rule is to facilitate the orderly transaction of business by an assembly.

2. The Majority Rules.

Speaking of the democratic process, Thomas Jefferson said that the first of all lessons in importance, but the last to be thoroughly learned, is "to consider the will of the society enounced by the majority of a single vote, as sacred as if unanimous."[2] When you join a deliberative assembly, you enter into an agreement with the other members to allow the will of the majority to prevail on all questions that come before the group. Abiding by this understanding that the majority rules is a fundamental part of what it means to be a member of a collective decision-making body. It takes no strength of character to yield to the will of the majority when the majority is voting your way. In parliamentary matters, nobody qualifies for the good sportsmanship trophy until he demonstrates that he can abide by the will of the majority whether he voted with them or not.

3. The Minority Must Not Be Suppressed.

Though the majority rules, its power is not absolute. If every member of an assembly save one were of the same opinion, the assembly would be no more justified in silencing that one, than he, if he had the power, would be in silencing the assembly.

The majority can limit or stop debate on any issue. It can reject the minority's position by voting against the issue. It can even prevent the consideration of a sensitive or objectionable issue with a two-thirds vote. But it must follow the rules that govern each of these procedures. For example, if a majority of two-thirds chooses to stop debate on an issue, debate stops for everybody. The majority cannot limit only the speeches of minority members. The majority also has no control over how an individual member casts his vote. It cannot make unanimous any vote that was not in fact unanimous. If a thousand members vote aye and a single member votes no, there is nothing the majority can do to keep that minority of one from voting as he chooses.

Under the rules of parliamentary procedure, a minority of even one member alone has the right to:

> Propose a motion, resolution, or amendment.
> Second a motion.
> Speak for or against any debatable question (unless some limitation on debate, which applies to all members, has been ordered).

Vote as he pleases.

Control the use of general consent and force a vote on any question.

Demand a rising vote.

Demand the *Division of a Question.*

Insist upon the enforcement of the assembly's rules by raising a *Point of Order.*

Insist that the presiding officer and the assembly follow the agenda by a *Call for the Orders of the Day.*

Prevent a unanimous vote.

Henry M. Robert summarized the balance between the rights of the majority and the minority this way:

> The great lesson for democracies to learn is for the majority to give to the minority a full, free opportunity to present their side of the case, and then for the minority, having failed to win a majority to their views, gracefully to submit and to recognize the action as that of the entire organization, and cheerfully to assist in carrying it out, until they can secure its repeal.[3]

4. Every Member Has the Right to Be Heard and to Hear What Other Members Have to Say.

Debate is the essential feature of a deliberative assembly. The very word *parliamentary* comes from the French word *parler* (English *parley*), which means to talk or discuss. Members can make a collective decision only when they have the opportunity to hear what they collectively have to say.

This principle is the reason that motions to limit or close debate require a two-thirds vote. The rules allow a full and free discussion of any debatable question until an overwhelming majority decides that they have finished deliberating and are ready to vote.

Permitting members to express dissenting views is not just fair; it's smart. You never know when the other side might be right! That is, you never know until they are allowed to speak. Only when all sides are freely heard can an assembly be sure it has made the best decision.

Our strongest opinions have no better safeguard to rest upon than a standing invitation to our opponents to prove them unfounded. If we are proven wrong in debate, we have the opportunity of exchanging error for truth. If we are proven right, the truth we contended for is more firmly established by its conquest over error.

5. All Members Have Equal Rights, Privileges, and Responsibilities.

Every member of an assembly has the right to participate in its proceedings. A member has the right to make motions, to speak in debate, to ask questions, and to vote. Unless the bylaws say otherwise, he has the right to nominate or to be nominated for office, to be named to a committee, or to exercise any other rights of membership. To deny to fellow members rights and privileges claimed for oneself is inequitable and unjust. He is a true gentleman, statesman, and Christian, who will fight as hard to preserve the rights of his most ardent opponent as he will his own. When he disagrees with other members, he may attack and rebut their ideas. But he must respect their right to speak and vote against his views as well.

The chairman especially must regard the equality of members while exercising the duties of the chair. No one expects a strong leader's views of his assembly's business to be nonpartisan, but he must preside with strict impartiality. He cannot play favorites. Every member must have an equal right and opportunity to debate, make motions, and participate in the assembly's business. Though the presiding officer may side with a particular faction, he cannot allow his own views to color his conduct while in the chair. He is there as a servant of the assembly, which means a servant of all the members collectively.

Members also have an equal responsibility to contribute to the business of their assembly. A top-heavy group in which the president and other officers are responsible for most of what gets done will never accomplish more than what those few strong leaders are able to do. The most effective organizations are those whose members take an active role in their own business.

6. Members Have the Right to Know What Is Going On.

Every member has the right to know what the pending question is and what effect it will have if adopted. Whenever the presiding officer states or puts a question, recognizes a member, makes a ruling, or announces an item of business, he must be clear. He must be sure that any member who is following the proceedings (and if he is really good, even those only half-way following the proceedings) knows exactly what is going on.

If you do not know what the pending question is, if you do not know what effect a motion would have if adopted, if you do not know whether a certain motion is in order, or if you have any other procedural question, then you have the right to ask the chair. Any member may direct a *Parliamentary Inquiry* (that is the technical name for procedural questions directed to the presiding officer) to the chair at any time, even when another member has the floor.

Where to Find *Your* Rules

This book is a general guide to the rules and procedures of meetings. It complies with general parliamentary law,

Robert's Rules of Order Newly Revised, and, for the most part, the other standard manuals of parliamentary procedure. Whatever I advise you to do here holds for all situations *except* those in which a particular rule of your assembly may tell you to do otherwise. To be effective in meetings of your church assembly, you must know both the general rules of procedure *and* the particular rules of your own assembly.

In order to conduct business, an assembly must have at least a written set of procedural rules to govern its proceedings. If it is a permanent organization, as opposed to a mass meeting of an unorganized ad hoc group, it must also have a set of bylaws that defines the organization's structure and function. The assembly may also incorporate, in which case it will have a corporate charter granted by the state. It may also have a set of standing rules or adopted policies that relate to the details of administering the assembly's business.

The following documents are the legal and parliamentary instruments that define and govern deliberative assemblies. They are listed in order of their authority. If a rule in a lower document conflicts with something in a higher, the rule in the higher document holds. Here is what you must have in hand to know the particular rules of your assembly:

The Bible

You are not likely to find references to the Bible in any other parliamentary manual, nor are you likely to find them in a legal guide to corporations. But I list it first here because church leaders need to be clear that the Bible stands above whatever human rules a religious assembly may choose to help them conduct their business. My home congregation addresses this issue in the preamble to our bylaws:

Whereas, the New Testament is the only perfect constitution for the doctrine, worship, discipline, and government of the Church, we accept it as our only rule of faith and practice. We acknowledge no creed, confession, or articles of faith other than the Word of God as recorded by the apostles and prophets of His Church.

These bylaws exist merely as a written understanding of how the principles of the New Testament shall be applied to the administration of this local congregation. If in any point there are found to be inconsistent with or contrary to the Christian Scriptures, they are, in that point, null and void.

However your church or agency chooses to address the relationship between the Bible and your parliamentary rules and legal documents, you need to be clear that the authority of the Bible is supreme. These other documents should govern only in those areas of opinion, application, and expediency where God himself has not legislated to the church.

Corporate Charter

If your church or agency is incorporated, it will have a *Corporate Charter* or *Articles of Incorporation* granted by the state. The contents of a corporate charter are determined by local statutes, which differ from state to state. The charter usually sets forth the name and purpose of the corporation, the number of directors, the names and addresses of the initial directors, and the names and addresses of the incorporators, and the address of the corporation's registered office. If your assembly incorporates as a nonprofit corporation, the charter should also meet the requirements of the Internal Revenue Service for establishing a tax-exempt, charitable institution.

A corporate charter should be drafted by an attorney licensed to practice in your state. Since the charter supersedes all other rules of the assembly, and since any amendment of the charter must comply with the statutory requirements of your state, the charter should contain only as much information as is necessary to obtain it. Leave as much as possible to your bylaws or other rules.

Bylaws

A *bylaw* is a self-imposed rule, adopted by an assembly, to conduct the assembly's business in a particular way. The bylaws usually prescribe the rights and duties of members, rules for the internal government of the assembly and the management of its affairs, and any other rules so important that they cannot be suspended or cannot be changed without previous notice and, usually, a two-thirds vote.

Every assembly has the right to enact whatever bylaws it deems necessary for the regulation of its own affairs. Though the actual number and content of bylaws will depend upon the size and nature of each assembly, the following bylaws articles are typical:

Article I. Name. This article sets forth the official name of the organization. If incorporated, the corporate charter will state the organization's name and this article can be omitted from the bylaws.

Article II. Purpose. This article, too, can usually be omitted for assemblies that have a corporate charter. Unincorporated societies should here state the purpose or purposes for which the assembly was formed. This article should be as general as possible, since an assembly may not consider business that is outside the statement of purpose in their bylaws or charter.

Article III. Members. The bylaws should state who is eli-

gible for membership in the assembly, how a person becomes a member, and any special requirements, duties, or
privileges of membership.

Article IV. Officers. Separate sections of this article
should name all officers by their proper titles and describe
their duties, qualifications, method of election, and terms
of office.

Article V. Meetings. The bylaws should fix the time and
place of regular meetings, state how and by whom special
meetings may be called, make provisions for an annual
meeting, and establish a quorum for all meetings.

*Article VI. Board of Directors (Elders, Deacons, Trust-
ees, etc.).* If the assembly has a governing board, then its
composition, duties, and powers should be carefully defined by the bylaws.

Article VII. Committees. The bylaws should also define
the composition, duties, and powers of each standing committee.

Article VIII. Parliamentary Authority. Most assemblies
adopt a standard manual of parliamentary procedure as
their parliamentary authority. This article can be a single
sentence that says: "The rules contained in the current
edition of *Robert's Rules of Order Newly Revised* shall
govern this assembly in all cases to which they are applicable and in which they are not inconsistent with these
bylaws and any special rules of order the assembly may
adopt."

Article IX. Amendment of Bylaws. Do not forget this
last article. Bylaws should always provide for their own
amendment. A standard wording for this article is: "These
bylaws may be amended at any regular meeting of the assembly by a two-thirds vote, provided that the amendment has been submitted in writing at the previous
regular meeting."

Some assemblies have their basic rules divided into a *Constitution and Bylaws*. The reason for this division is to make some of the rules more difficult to amend. The most fundamental provisions would go in the constitution and the lesser rules in the bylaws. The practice of having a separate constitution and bylaws is becoming less common as assemblies find that keeping all the rules relating to each subject under one article within a single document is less confusing and produces a more workable set of rules.

Rules of Order

Most of an assembly's *rules of order* are usually contained in its adopted *parliamentary authority*. It can, however, adopt additional rules to supplement or modify those in its parliamentary authority.

Special rules of order supersede those contained in an adopted parliamentary authority. If there is a conflict between a special rule of order and the assembly's parliamentary authority, the special rule of order is applied. For example, *Robert's Rules of Order Newly Revised* permits each member to speak twice in debate on a given question for ten minutes each time. Your assembly could adopt a rule limiting speeches to three minutes each. When a group adopts a special rule of order, it does not toss out its parliamentary authority altogether. It is still in force. It simply is not applicable to cases governed by special rules of order.

Like bylaws, rules of order may be adopted by previous notice and a two-thirds vote. But unlike bylaws, rules of order can be suspended by a motion to *Suspend the Rules*.

Standing Rules

The basic difference between *rules of order* and *standing rules* is that rules of order relate to procedural matters in meetings and standing rules relate to general administrative policies of the assembly. Standing rules can be adopted or suspended by a majority vote, without previous notice, at any business meeting.

How Important Is Parliamentary Procedure to Your Church Business Meetings?

Your church business meetings will be governed by some set of rules. They might not be written down. They might be made up as you go along. They might ignore the wisdom and experience passed down through centuries of parliamentary law. They might be illegal or unscriptural or just plain unfair. But your meetings will be conducted by somebody's stated or unstated rules of procedure. The only question is how fair, efficient, and legal those rules will be.

The best way to avoid a misunderstanding is to have an understanding. When chairmen and members know and conduct themselves in accordance with the customary rules and courtesies of parliamentary procedure, there are fewer misunderstandings.

My plea is that those who are charged with doing the Father's business make good use of the rules and customs that experience has shown best enable a group of persons to discuss and determine a course of action to be taken by the group. Of all people, Christians should be most eager to see their affairs conducted in a fair, efficient, and orderly manner. Hence the need for church leaders to have a working knowledge of parliamentary procedure.

Churches do the most important business in the world. When the president of the United States convenes his cabinet or the chairman of General Motors calls his board to order, no one's soul hangs in the balance. But when churches meet to do their business, the eternal destiny of

people is at stake. To the church alone God has committed
the great task of saving souls and making disciples. There
is no more important business in the world than that. It
behooves us to do it as well as we can.

Notes

1. There are a several editions of *Robert's Rules* in print. If
your assembly's bylaws prescribe *"Robert's Rules of Order"* or
"the current edition of *Robert's Rules of Order*" as your parliamentary authority, be sure that you have in hand the *Robert's
Rules of Order Newly Revised* published by Scott, Foresman
and Company. It supersedes all previous editions of *Robert's
Rules*. As of this writing, the current edition was published in
1990.

2. Thomas Jefferson, Letter to Baron von Humboldt, 1817,
as cited by Alice Sturgis, *Sturgis Standard Code of Parliamentary Procedure*, 2nd ed. (New York: McGraw-Hill, 1966), p. 131.

3. Henry M. Robert, *Parliamentary Law* (New York: Ir-
vington Publishers, 1975), p. 4.

2
Basic Procedure

Your church has been without a preacher for three months. Scores of resumes, interviews, and trial sermons have failed to produce a suitable candidate. The pulpit committee has called a special meeting for this evening to report to the church on the search for a new minister.

You are convinced the church should call Dr. C. G. Presley, the retired Bible college professor who has filled the pulpit for the past three months. Though most of the pulpit committee thinks the church needs a younger man, the congregation loves Dr. Presley and you believe his wisdom and experience are just what the church needs right now. You wish someone would propose that the congregation call Dr. Presley to be the new minister, but you have never spoken up in a business meeting before and you are not exactly sure how to go about it. You could wait and see if someone who knows how to get things done in a meeting proposes your idea, or you could blunder in as best you can and hope your proposal goes through. Both alternatives are, at best, uncertain. Isn't there a better way?

Yes, there is. The solution to your problem is simple. You need to know how to handle the basic tool of a deliberative assembly: the *motion*.

All business in a deliberative assembly is conducted by acting on motions. A motion is a formal proposal that the assembly say or do something. An assembly *acts* by adopting a motion that orders the desired action. It *speaks* by adopting a motion that states its views (motions that state views are called *resolutions*). Since motions are the only means for conducting business in a meeting, they are the most important tools of parliamentary procedure. If you want to influence the decisions of your group, you must understand how to introduce, consider, and dispose of motions.

The usual process for handling a motion involves six steps: (1) A member *makes* the motion. (2) Another member *seconds* it. (3) The chair *states the question* on the motion. (4) The members *debate* it. (5) The chair *puts the question* to a vote. (6) The chair *announces the result* of the vote.

Step One: A Member *Makes* the Motion.

You must be recognized by the chair in order to *make* a motion. When no other business is pending and no other speaker has the floor, you should stand and address the chair. Wait for the chair to recognize you. A presiding officer usually recognizes a member by calling the person's name or pointing to him. In large assemblies, such as a convention, the chair may call out the number of your microphone. Once the chair recognizes you, everyone else must be seated while you make your motion. For example:

> MEMBER: "Mr. Chairman."
> CHAIR: "The chair recognizes Mr. Smith."
> MEMBER: "I move that _____."

As soon as you have made your motion, sit down and wait for the motion to be seconded, then stated by the chair. A motion cannot be debated until the chair states it to the assembly. Do not attempt to explain or argue for your motion just yet. The maker of a motion has the right to speak first in debate on that motion, so you need not worry about losing the floor if you sit while the motion is seconded and stated.

Motions should be worded as clearly and as exactly as possible. Motions that are unclear or needlessly complex will confuse the assembly and make the chances of their adoption slim. Be sure to word your motion so that the chair and the assembly know exactly what you want them to do. Use the exact parliamentary language your motion calls for. If your motion is longer than one sentence, write it down. Make two copies. Keep one and send the other copy to the chair.

Step Two: Another Member *Seconds* the Motion.

Most motions require a *second* in order to be considered. A member may second a motion without being recognized by the chair. Usually a member who wishes to have the question considered will quickly say:

> MEMBER: "I second the motion."
> Or,
> "Second."

If no one seconds your motion, it cannot be considered by the assembly. The chair handles such cases this way:

> CHAIR: "Is there a second? . . . *(Pause)* . . . If there is no second the motion will not be considered. . . . *(Pause again, no response)* . . . There is no second. The motion will not be considered. The next item of business is . . . ."

The purpose of a second is to inform the chair whether or not more than one member wishes to take up that motion. A second does not imply that the seconder favors the motion, but only that he agrees that the motion should come before the assembly. You may second a motion because you want your group to go on record as rejecting it.

A motion made by a board or committee does not require a second, because the motion obviously has the support of more than one member already.

The chart of motions inside the front of the book will show you which motions do and which do not require a second.

Step Three: The Chair *States the Question* on the Motion.

After another member seconds your motion, the chair formally places it before the assembly by *stating the question* on the motion. Using the exact wording you used in making the motion, the chair states the question to the assembly as follows:

CHAIR: "It has been moved and seconded that
_____. Is there any discussion?"
Or,
"It has been moved and seconded that
_____.
Are you ready for the question?"

The phrase "Are you ready for the question?" is an older parliamentary form. Most chairmen now use "Is there any discussion?" Either phrase signals the members that the question is now open for debate.

If a motion is undebatable, the chair omits the words "Is there any discussion?" and proceeds to put the question to a vote.

If a written resolution or motion was clearly read by the member who offered it or if everyone has a printed copy, the chair may state the question this way:

CHAIR: "It has been moved and seconded to adopt the resolution just read. Is there any discussion?"

Or,

"The question is on the adoption of Recommendation Number Three as printed on page 97 of your Convention Program. Is there any discussion?"

Your motion now belongs to the assembly. Up until the chair states the question, you have the exclusive right to modify or withdraw your motion. But once the chair states the question, it can be amended or withdrawn only with the assembly's consent.

If your motion is in order, the chair must state the question on it immediately. If the motion is out of order, the chair does not state the question, but rules the motion out of order with a brief explanation. For example:

CHAIR: "The chair rules that the motion is out of order because it calls for endorsing a political candidate, which Bylaw Three forbids us to do."

Or,

"Amendments are not in order at this time."

Or,

"The member's motion is out of order. A main motion is already pending."

If the chair rules your motion out of order, you may appeal his ruling, in which case the assembly will decide to sustain or overturn his ruling. Do not appeal the ruling, though, unless you have good reason to believe the chair is mistaken.

In ruling a motion out of order, the chair should be clear

that it is the motion and not the member that is out of order. Ruling a member out of order means that he is guilty of misconduct in the meeting.

After your motion has been stated by the chair, it is *pending* until adopted, rejected, or disposed of in some other way. A pending motion is also called a *question*.

Step Four: The Members *Debate* the Motion.

Once your motion is before the assembly, members have the right to debate it, if it is debatable. If a motion is neither debatable nor amendable, the chair skips this step and proceeds to put the motion to a vote. If an undebatable motion is amendable, the chair allows amendments, but no speeches, to be made at this time. If the motion is debatable, the chair should turn toward the maker of the motion to see if he wishes to speak to his motion.

Claim your right as the maker the motion to speak first in debate. After you have spoken, the chair should, as far as possible, let the floor alternate between those favoring the motion and those opposing it.

Something else can happen to your motion during debate. The members may decide they don't want to be restricted to simply adopting or rejecting your motion as originally presented. They may choose to amend it, postpone it to a later time, refer it to a committee, or lay it on the table to take care of some more urgent matter. All of these actions are taken by adopting one of the subsidiary motions, which are explained in the next chapter.

Whether you want to speak for or against the pending question or move one of the subsidiary motions just mentioned, you must be recognized by the chair in order to speak. Each member has the right to speak twice on the same motion for up to ten minutes each time, unless the rules of the assembly or a motion to *Limit or Extend De-*

bate say otherwise. No member may make a second speech, however, so long as any member who has not yet spoken on that motion seeks the floor.

You must address your remarks to the presiding officer, maintain a courteous tone, and speak only to the immediately pending question. The chairman should remain seated while you are speaking and, as long as you obey the rules and no disorder arises, the chairman may not interrupt you.

Debate proceeds until every member who desires to speak has spoken, the assembly closes debate by ordering the *Previous Question,* or a preset time for debate expires. There is a further discussion of debate in Chapter 4.

Step Five: The Chair *Puts the Question* to a Vote.

When debate has ended, the chair rises and *puts the question* to a vote. To do this, he stands, restates the question, and calls for the affirmative then the negative vote. No matter how unanimous the affirmative vote appears to be, the chair must always give opponents of a motion the opportunity to vote against it.

Methods of Voting

The form for putting the question differs according to the method of voting used. The common forms and when they are used are:

Voice Vote. A voice vote is the usual method of voting on motions that require a simple majority. The chair takes a voice vote by saying:

CHAIR: "The question is on adoption of the motion to
　　　　＿＿＿＿. As many as are in favor of the mo-
　　　　tion, say 'aye'. . . . *(Pause for response)* . . .

Those opposed, say 'no' . . . *(Pause for response)*."

Rising Vote. A rising vote is the usual method of voting on motions that require a two-thirds vote. It is also used when the chair or a member believes the result of a voice vote was inconclusive. The chair takes a rising vote by saying:

CHAIR: "The question is on adoption of the motion to _____. Those in favor of the motion will stand. . . . Be seated. . . . Those opposed will stand. . . . Be seated."

A single member, by calling for a *Division of the Assembly,* can compel the chairman to take a rising vote. But he cannot compel the chair to count the vote unless the assembly adopts a motion to take a counted vote. If the chair believes that a rising vote is inconclusive, he can on his own initiative order that the vote be counted. The form for taking a counted vote is:

CHAIR: "The question is on adoption of the motion to _____. Those in favor of the motion will stand and remain standing until counted. . . . Be seated. . . . Those opposed will stand and remain standing until counted. . . . Be seated."

In a small meeting, the chairman may count the vote himself. He may ask the secretary to verify his count if he wishes. In large assemblies, the chair should appoint tellers to count the vote.

Show of Hands. In smaller assemblies and committee meetings, a show of hands may take the place of a rising vote. In some conventions, delegates vote by raising their ballots or credentials. The question is put by a show of hands as follows:

> CHAIR: "The question is on _____. Those in favor of the motion will raise their hands. . . . Lower your hands. . . . Those opposed will raise their hands. . . . Lower your hands."

Ballot Vote. Voting by marking a written or printed ballot allows members to express their decisions without revealing how they voted. It is also the most accurate method of counting votes in large assemblies and conventions. A ballot vote may be taken when it is ordered by the assembly or is prescribed by its rules.

The presiding officer, the secretary, or the chairman of the tellers should instruct the members on how to cast their ballots. The following example is for marking a printed ballot with a pen.

> CHAIR: "The question is on _____. To vote in favor of the motion, put an X in the box marked yes. To vote against the motion, put an X in the box marked no."

General Consent. Routine or noncontroversial actions may be taken without a formal vote. If you think no one in the meeting will object to your proposal, you may ask for *general consent*—sometimes called *unanimous consent*—that the action be taken. The procedure is as follows:

> MEMBER: "Mr. Chairman, I ask unanimous consent that _____ *(stating the action to be taken)."*
>
> CHAIR: "If there is no objection, then _____ *(stating the action to be taken).* . . .

(Pause) . . . Without objection, it is so ordered."

If any member objects, the motion must be formally stated, debated, and put to a vote in the regular manner. An objection to taking an action by general consent does not necessarily imply that the objecting member opposes the proposed action. The objection applies only to the action's being taken without a formal vote.

General consent is a useful tool for streamlining an assembly's business, but it should never be used to railroad proposals through a meeting, and you should not hesitate to object to the procedure when you think it unjustified.

Types of Votes

Most actions of a deliberative assembly require a *majority vote*. The word *majority* means "more than half." Unless your assembly's rules say otherwise, a majority vote is defined as "more than half of the legal votes cast." Only the actual votes cast are used to compute a majority. Abstentions are not counted because nothing may be presumed of members who do not vote except that they have consented to allow the members who do vote to decide the question for the group.

It is possible for only one vote to constitute a majority. If, in a meeting of 100 members, one member voted "aye," no one voted "no," and 99 members abstained, that single affirmative vote is a majority of the legal votes cast and is sufficient to adopt a motion.

Some actions require a *two-thirds vote*. The term means "at least two-thirds of the legal votes cast." For a motion requiring a two-thirds vote to pass there must be twice as many affirmative votes as there are negative votes. A quick method of computing a two-thirds vote is to double the negative vote. If the affirmative vote is that number or higher, you have a two-thirds vote.

A *tie-vote* is a vote that is equally divided between the affirmative and the negative. A tie vote is *not* a deadlock. It has the same effect as a negative vote. Since a majority is more than half, a motion on which there is a tie vote has failed to receive more than half and is lost.

Unless an assembly's rules say otherwise, the chairman may choose to break a tie by voting in the affirmative, but, like any other member, he may abstain and allow the motion to be defeated. The chair could also affect the result of a vote by *creating* a tie. If the vote on a motion were 50 ayes and 49 noes, which is a majority, the chair could defeat the motion by voting in the negative to create a tie, in which case the motion would no longer have a majority and would be lost.

Step Six: The Chair *Announces the Result* of the Vote.

The chair announces the result of the vote immediately after putting the question, except when the assembly is waiting for the count of a ballot vote. To announce the result of a vote the chair does four things:

(1) Says which side "has it."
(2) Declares that the motion is carried or lost.
(3) States the effect of the vote or orders its execution.
(4) States the question on the next motion to be voted on or announces the next item of business.

The last two parts of the announcement will differ, depending on the particular motion and the circumstances under which it is made. The form for the first two parts of the announcement depends upon the vote required and the method of voting.

The result of the various types of votes is announced as follows:

Voice Vote

CHAIR: "The ayes (noes) have it and the motion is adopted (lost)." *(Unless the effect of the motion is obvious, the chair should here state the effect of the vote or order its execution. This applies to the other methods of voting as well.)*

Rising Majority Vote

CHAIR: "The affirmative (negative) has it and the motion is adopted (lost). . . ."

Rising Two-Thirds Vote

CHAIR: "There are (are less than) two-thirds in the affirmative and the motion is adopted (lost)."

Counted Majority Vote (whether by ballot or counted otherwise)

CHAIR: "There are 51 in the affirmative and 48 in the negative. The affirmative has it and the motion is adopted. . . ."

Or,

"There are 30 in the affirmative and 55 in the negative. The negative has it and the motion is lost. . . ."

Counted Two-Thirds Vote

CHAIR: "There are 61 in the affirmative and 30 in the negative. There are two-thirds in the affirmative and the motion is adopted. . . ."

Or,

"There are 55 in the affirmative and 45 in the negative. There are less than two-thirds in the affirmative and the motion is lost. . . ."

Counted Majority Vote When the Chair Makes or Breaks a Tie

CHAIR: "There are 30 in the affirmative and 30 in the negative. The chair votes in the affirmative, making 31 in the affirmative and 30 in the negative. The affirmative has it and the motion is adopted. . . ."

Or,

"There are 30 in the affirmative and 29 in the negative. The chair votes in the negative, making 30 in the affirmative and 30 in the negative. The affirmative and the negative are tied and the motion is lost. . . ."

Counted Two-Thirds Vote When the Chair's Vote Affects the Result '

CHAIR: "There are 59 in the affirmative and 30 in the negative. The chair votes in the affirmative, making 60 in the affirmative and 30 in the negative. There are two-thirds in the affirmative and the motion is adopted. . . ."

Or,

"There are 60 in the affirmative and 30 in the negative. The chair votes in the negative, making 60 in the affirmative and 31 in the negative. There are less than two-thirds in the affirmative and the motion is lost. . . ."

In all but a counted vote, the result is determined by the chair's judgment alone. If the chair believes a voice vote to be inconclusive, he may order a rising vote. If a rising vote remains inconclusive, he may order a counted vote.

If you doubt the result of a vote, call for a *Division of the Assembly* or move that a counted vote be taken.

You have the right to change your vote up to the time the chair announces the result. After that, you must request the assembly's permission to change your vote. No one, however, may interrupt the chairman while he is actually taking a vote.

The six steps in handling a motion are illustrated by the following example of the introduction, consideration, and adoption of a *main motion.*

MEMBER 1: *(Rising and addressing the chair)* "Mr. Chairman."

CHAIR: "The chair recognizes Brother Smith."

MEMBER 1: "Mr. Chairman, I move that the church call Dr. C. G. Presley to be our new preacher."

MEMBER 2: *(Without rising)* "I second the motion."

CHAIR: "It has been moved and seconded that the church call Dr. C. G. Presley to be our new preacher. Is there any discussion?"

MEMBER 1: *(Again rising to address the chair)* "Mr. Chairman."

CHAIR: "Brother Smith."

MEMBER 1: "Mr. Chairman, I believe the church should extend a call to Dr. Presley because . . . ."

. . . .

CHAIR: *(After no other member claims the floor for debate)* "The question is on the motion to call Dr. Presley to be our new preacher. As many as are in favor of the motion, say aye. . . . *(Pause for response)* . . . Those opposed, say no . . . *(Pause for response)* . . . The ayes have it and the motion is adopted. The church clerk will immediately give Dr. Presley written notice that the church has extended to him a call to be our new preacher. The next item of business is . . ."

Summary

Whatever else you may learn about parliamentary procedure you *must* thoroughly understand these six basic steps in handling a motion. An assembly can act or speak only by adopting motions. Every motion made in a meeting must go through this process. If you want to be able to do things in a meeting, learn it well.

3
Motions

You now know how to make a motion in a meeting and what happens to it once you make it. But you are not quite ready to be turned loose on your board of deacons, ladies auxiliary, or church convention. In this chapter we'll discuss the rest of what you need to know about using motions.

There is more than one kind of motion. *Robert's Rules* lists 82 different motions that can be made in a meeting. This discussion will be limited to 23 of these. You should know four things about each motion:

1. What class of motion it is.
2. The purpose of the motion.
3. Its order of precedence.
4. The basic rules governing its use.

1. What Class of Motion Is It?

Motions are divided into five classes: *main motions, subsidiary motions, privileged motions, incidental motions,* and *restorative motions.* Each motion's purpose and characteristics determine its class. A few motions can belong to either of two classes depending upon the circumstances under which they are made. We'll point them out when we come to them.

Main Motions

Main motions are the most important because they introduce business to the assembly. Any subject or substantive proposal—as opposed to a procedural question—comes before the meeting by way of a main motion. Because main motions introduce subjects, and parliamentary rules permit an assembly to consider only one subject at a time, once a main motion is introduced, no other main motion is in order until the first one has been disposed of.

Novices to parliamentary procedure are usually eager for the first chance to try out any fancy procedural motions they learn. That is understandable. After only a few hours of study you, too, can be the first kid on your block to *Call for the Orders of the Day* or *Fix the Time to Which to Adjourn*. Though you should learn what those motions do and when they are used, do not forget that the business of a deliberative assembly is to conduct business, not to tie up the time and energy of its members with procedural questions. Main motions are the vehicles of an assembly's business. The other motions are there to escort the main motions through the parliamentary process.

Though the subsidiary, privileged, and incidental motions are usually made while a main motion is pending, several of them can be made and adopted while no main motion is pending. For example, a member could, while no main motion is pending, move to *Limit Debate* to two minutes per speaker for the duration of a meeting. Or, a member could move to *Postpone to a Certain Time* or *Refer to Committee* some matter that is not then pending. In these cases, when any of the special procedural motions are made while no main motion is pending or if they are made in reference to some item of business that is not then pending, they are treated as main motions. They are amendable, debatable, cannot interrupt a speaker, and can be made only when no other main motion is pending. *Robert's Rules of Order Newly Revised* places these motions, when made under the conditions described, in a special classification called *Incidental Main Motions.*

The main thing you need to know is that when one of the procedural motions is made while nothing else is pending, or if it is applied to a motion that is not then pending, it is a main motion.

Subsidiary Motions

Subsidiary motions assist an assembly in disposing of main motions. There are seven of them:

> Lay on the Table
> Previous Question
> Limit or Extend Debate
> Postpone to a Certain Time
> Refer to Committee
> Amend
> Postpone Indefinitely

The usefulness of subsidiary motions can be illustrated by the following example. Suppose you had to immediately accept or reject this proposal: Resolved, That we throw out the baby and the bath water. Answer yes or no, time is up. Of course, for baby's sake, refusing the proposal is the lesser of two evils, but you're still stuck with the dirty bath water. A better solution would be to reword the proposal so that by saying yes you could keep the baby and toss the water.

Likewise, it is unwise to force a deliberative assembly to immediately adopt or reject every main motion that comes before it. Subsidiary motions give an assembly a wider range of choices on what they can do with a main motion. By adopting one of the subsidiary .motions, an assembly can reword, study, interrupt consideration of, or delay their decision on a main motion.

Privileged Motions

None of the five privileged motions has anything to do with pending questions. They are emergency motions that deal with matters of such importance (such as getting to go home!) that they are allowed to interrupt the consideration of anything else. The privileged motions are:

> Fix the Time to Which to Adjourn
> Adjourn
> Recess
> Question of Privilege
> Call for the Orders of the Day

Incidental Motions

Incidental motions take care of certain procedural matters that arise while handling business in a meeting. Most of them are undebatable and must be decided immediately. For example, if a member believes the chair has made an error or has failed to enforce a rule, he may raise a *Point of Order* to point out the breech of the rules. If a member doubts the result of a voice vote, he may call for a *Division of the Assembly*. Both of these incidental motions deal with procedural matters, and both have to be decided before whatever business they interrupted can continue. The incidental motions you should know how to use are:

> Point of Order
> Appeal
> Parliamentary Inquiry
> Point of Information

Division of the Assembly
Division of a Question
Suspend the Rules.

Restorative Motions

In most cases, decisions made in a meeting are meant to be final. But there needs to be room for exceptions. This class of motions provides assemblies with a means for undoing what they have done.

Robert's Rules of Order Newly Revised calls this class of motions *Motions That Bring a Question Again Before the Assembly*. That is precisely what they do, but that label is a bit long. I prefer the term *restorative motions* to describe this class. They "restore" by bringing back for further consideration a motion that was before the assembly and was disposed of. Restorative motions allow an assembly to reconsider a matter voted on earlier in the same meeting, take up something previously laid on the table or referred to a committee, or change something previously adopted and still in force. The most frequently used motions in this classification are:

Reconsider
Rescind or Amend Something Previously
    Adopted
Take From the Table

2. What Is the Purpose of the Motion?

The most useful thing to know about any motion is what it does. To get the most from your study of parliamentary procedure, learn to match motions with purposes and purposes with motions.

For example, if you have made a main motion, you need to know that a member who moves to *Postpone Indefi-*

nitely is trying to kill your motion. You should also remember to use that same motion when someone else makes a motion you want to defeat.

3. What Is the Order of Precedence of the Motion?

Precedence is the parliamentary term for the rank of a motion. Every motion has a rank or order of precedence that determines when it can be introduced, considered, and put to a vote. The order of precedence for the thirteen motions with an assigned rank is:

> *Privileged Motions*
> 1. Fix the Time to Which to Adjourn
> 2. Adjourn
> 3. Recess
> 4. Question of Privilege
> 5. Call for the Orders of the Day
>
> *Subsidiary Motions*
> 6. Lay on the Table
> 7. Previous Question
> 8. Limit or Extend Debate
> 9. Postpone to a Certain Time
> 10. Refer to Committee
> 11. Amend
> 12. Postpone Indefinitely
> 13. THE MAIN MOTION

Motions at the top of the list have a higher rank than motions at the bottom and are said to *take precedence* over them. For example, main motions have the lowest rank, so they take precedence over no other motion. You cannot make a main motion if anything else, even another main motion, is pending. The motion to *Adjourn*, however, has such a high rank that it takes precedence over all but one other motion. That means that no matter how many other motions are pending, the members can always vote to adjourn and go home when they want.

The basic rule of precedence is that when the assembly is considering a particular motion, any motion of a higher rank may be proposed, but no motion of lower rank may be proposed. It is like bids at an auction. The bid can always go up, but never down.

Suppose a member proposes a main motion "That the church donate five hundred dollars to the American Bible Society to send Bibles to Latin America." During debate on that motion, another member moves to amend it by striking the words "five hundred" and inserting the words "one thousand." The amendment is in order because the motion to *Amend* has a higher rank than the main motion and takes precedence over it. Once the amendment is stated by the chair and becomes the pending question, a motion to *Postpone Indefinitely* would be out of order because it has a lower rank than the motion to *Amend*. But a higher ranking motion, such as *Refer to Committee* would be in order.

When several motions are pending, they are voted on in the reverse order that they were proposed. In our example above, the motion to *Refer* would be the *immediately pending question*. It would be the first motion put to a vote. If the assembly rejects it and the main motion does not go to a committee, the chair then puts the question on the amendment. Then he puts the question on the main motion as amended or not.

When I preside at a meeting or serve as parliamentarian, I use a legal pad to keep track of pending motions. In our example my pad would look like this:

REFER: To missions committee.

AMEND: Strike "$500" and insert "$1,000."

MAIN MOTION: That the church donate $500 to the ABS to send Bibles to Latin America.

Refer is at the top because it was the last motion made and is the immediately pending question. It will be the first motion put to a vote. The amendment comes next, and the main motion last.

The order of precedence for incidental and for restorative motions is a bit different. Since incidental motions take care of certain procedural matters that arise while handling business, they must be decided as soon as they are made. Therefore they do not need to have an assigned rank. They simply take precedence over any immediately pending question they were needed to solve.

Restorative motions are actually special kinds of main motions. With the exception of the motion to *Reconsider,* which has its own special rules. restorative motions take precedence over nothing and can be made and considered only while no other business is pending.

4. What Are the Basic Rules Governing the Use of This Motion?

You should know these basic rules about each motion: (1) Can it interrupt a speaker? (2) Does it require a second? (3) Is it amendable? (4) Is it debatable? (5) What vote is required to adopt it?

The chart on *Rules and Precedence of Motions* in the front of the book will answer those five questions for each motion and tell you their classification and order of precedence. Some of the motions have rules that are peculiar to them, which will be discussed in the next section about individual motions.

The basic rules governing motions are logical. If you know the purpose of a motion, you can usually figure out the rules that apply to it. The following guidelines should help you:

(1) Can the motion interrupt a speaker? He can be interrupted for a matter that has a definite time limit, such as a *Point of Order* or a motion to *Reconsider,* or for something that concerns the needs of the assembly as a whole, such as a *Question of Privilege* concerning the assembly or a *Call for the Orders of the Day.*

(2) Does the motion require a second? Most motions require a second. Actions that a member has the right to request or demand, such as a *Point of Order* or a *Division of the Assembly,* do not require a second.

(3) Is the motion amendable? If a motion can be made in more than one form, it is amendable. If it cannot, it is not.

(4) Is the motion debatable? A motion is debatable unless it is a simple procedural matter that you either do or do not do and can be understood by members without debate, such as a motion to *Adjourn, Recess,* or *Take from the Table.*

(5) What vote is required to adopt the motion? A simple majority is enough to adopt most motions. A two-thirds vote is required for actions that limit the rights of members, such as the *Previous Question* or *Limit Debate.*

Purpose, Description, and Form
for Making Motions

This section details the purpose, description, and form for making each of the subsidiary, privileged, incidental, and restorative motions. Since I have already described main motions as a class and have given a detailed example of how they are handled in Chapter 2, I do not discuss them again here.

Under each motion is an example or examples of how to use that motion. Pay close attention to who says what and when, since you cannot actually make the motion unless you know what to say. In some cases, where some peculiar parliamentary language is used, I also tell you what the chair says in handling the motion.

Postpone Indefinitely

Purpose and Description. *Postpone Indefinitely* suppresses or kills a main motion without permitting it to come to a direct vote. Postponing a motion indefinitely has the same effect as a negative vote on it.

This motion is one of the exceptions to the rule that members can debate only the immediately pending question. Since *Postpone Indefinitely* finally disposes of a main motion, debate on it can go into the merits of the main motion to which it is applied.

The motion offers three tactical advantages to opponents of a main motion. First,it gives them two chances to defeat the motion they oppose. Second, it doubles their opportunity to speak against it, since a member who has exhausted his right to debate the main question can speak again on the motion to *Postpone Indefinitely.* Third, it enables opponents to gage the strength of opposition to a motion within the assembly.

Example.

MEMBER: "I move that the question be postponed indefinitely."

Amend

Purpose and Description. *Amend* is the most useful and most used subsidiary motion. Its purpose is to change the wording of another motion. It is usually applied to a main motion but can be used to modify any amendable motion. The motion to *Amend* can itself be amended.

There are four ways to amend a motion: by striking out words, by adding or inserting words, by striking out and inserting words, or by adopting a substitute motion. When you make an amendment, say exactly what you want to do to the motion you are amending.

Amendments must be germane to the question to which they are applied. That is, they must in some way involve the same issue as the motion to be amended. They can be hostile to the spirit of the original motion but cannot make adoption of the amended motion equivalent to rejection of the original motion. Amendments are also out of order if they attempt to change one kind of procedural motion into another. For example, you could not strike the words "refer to the finance committee" from a motion and insert "postpone indefinitely."

Examples. Suppose the following main motion is pending: "That the church donate five hundred dollars to the American Bible Society to send Bibles to Latin America." The motion could be amended in any of the following ways:

Amendment by adding or inserting:

MEMBER: "I move to amend the main motion by adding the words 'and to Poland.'"

Amendment by striking out:

MEMBER: "I move to amend the main motion by striking the words 'to send Bibles to Latin America.'"

Amendment by striking out and inserting:

MEMBER: "I move to amend the main motion by striking out the words 'five hundred' and inserting the word 'one thousand.'"

Amendment by substitution:

MEMBER: "I move to amend the main motion by substituting the following motion: 'That the church add the American Bible Society to the agencies supported by our missions program.'"

In the last example, the desired change was substantial enough that it was simpler to substitute rather than tinker with the text of the original motion. When an amendment is proposed through a substitute motion, both the main motion and the proposed substitute are perfected by any other amendments members wish to make to them. Then a vote is taken on whether to accept the proposed substitute. Finally, the assembly votes on adopting the final motion, which may be either the substitute or the original main motion.

Refer to Committee

Purpose and Description. The motion to *Refer* sends a pending question to a committee. Motions are usually referred so that a committee may study the question and return it to the assembly with recommendations. Occasionally an assembly delegates to the committee the duty of deciding and carrying out the proposal. Instructions to the committee may be made as part of the motion to *Refer.* Any amendments pending when a main motion is referred go with it to the committee.

See Chapter 6 for a fuller treatment of committees.

Examples.

MEMBER: "I move to refer the motion to the Missions Committee."

Or,

"I move to refer the motion to a committee of five to be appointed by the Chair,
with instructions to report at the next
congregational meeting."

Or,

"I move to refer the pending motion to a
committee consisting of Mr. Campbell,
Mr. Stone, and Mr. Scott, with full power
to act for the assembly in this matter."

Your motion to *Refer to Committee* may be as specific as
you wish. If you move to refer a motion to a standing committee, give the committee instructions on exactly what
they are to do with the motion and when they are to report
back to the assembly. If you move to refer a motion to a
special committee, seize the initiative by naming the
chairman and members of the committee. This way you
entrust the pending motion to those members whom you
believe will best handle the matter.

Postpone to a Certain Time

Purpose and Description. *Postpone to a Certain Time*
delays consideration of a pending question until a certain
time or until after a certain event. A motion may be postponed to a later time in the same meeting or to a later
meeting. Do not confuse this motion with *Postpone Indefinitely,* which kills the main motion to which it is applied.

When a main motion is postponed to a particular time,
it becomes a *general order* for that time. If no other business is pending when that time arrives, the chair will state

the postponed motion to the assembly for consideration. If some other business is pending, the chair will state the motion as soon as the pending item of business is handled.

A main motion may also be postponed and made a *special order.* Special orders interrupt whatever business is pending when the time for their consideration arrives. Because they interrupt, it takes a two-thirds vote to postpone a main motion and make it a special order.

The highest possible priority that can be assigned to a postponed motion is to make it *The Special Order* for a meeting, which is different from *a special order.* The Special Order for a meeting is taken up immediately after the reading and approval of the minutes. No other business is in order until The Special Order for that meeting has been disposed of. Only one item of business can be The Special Order for a given meeting.

Whether a postponed motion becomes a general order, a special order, or The Special Order for a meeting, depends on how important the assembly thinks that item of business is and how high a priority the members wish to give its consideration. See the section on special orders in Chapter 5.

Examples.

MEMBER: "I move to postpone the motion to the next meeting."

Or,

"I move to postpone the question until one o'clock."

Or,

"I move to postpone the question and make it a special order for eight o'clock at the next regular meeting."

Limit or Extend Debate

Purpose and Description. This motion enables an assembly to control debate by setting or extending a time limit for discussion of a pending question or of debate in general. A motion to *Limit Debate* may reduce the number or length of speeches, or the total time allotted for debate on a motion. A motion to *Extend Debate* can be applied to limitations on debate imposed by the regular rules or by a previous order to *Limit Debate*.

Because it suspends the rules and restricts the basic right of members to participate in discussion of an issue, the motion to *Limit or Extend Debate* requires a two-thirds vote for adoption.

Examples.

MEMBER: "I move to limit debate on this motion to three minutes per speaker."

Or,

"I move to limit debate on this motion to ten minutes."

Or,

"I move to limit debate on this motion to the next four speakers recognized by the Chair."

Or,

"I move to extend the time for consideration of the pending question by ten minutes."

Previous Question

Purpose and Description. A better name for this motion would be *Vote Immediately*. It has nothing to do with any question previously considered by the assembly. The old English name, introduced in Parliament in 1604, just happens to be one of the anachronisms of parliamentary procedure.

The *Previous Question* is the motion used to immediately close debate and bring one or more pending questions to a vote. It also has the effect of preventing the making of any further subsidiary motions, except *Lay on the Table,* which has a higher rank than *Previous Question.*

The *Previous Question* can be ordered on the immediately pending motion or on a series of pending motions. Unless it is qualified in some way, the *Previous Question* applies only to the immediately pending motion.

Examples.

MEMBER: "I move the previous question."
Or,
"I move to vote immediately."
Or,
"I call for the question."
Or,
"I move the previous question on all pending motions."
Or,
"I move the previous question on all pending subsidiary motions."

The chair states the question on the *Previous Question* as follows:

CHAIR: "It has been moved and seconded to order the previous question."
Or,
"It has been moved and seconded to order the previous question on all pending motions (or however the motion was qualified)."

If the motion is adopted, the assembly is then said to be under *an order for the Previous Question.*

If a member uses the popular, but incorrect wording "I call for the question," the chair should treat that as a motion to order the *Previous Question.* But the chair should ignore or call to order members who cry "Question!" or "Call for the question!" from their seats while another member is speaking or seeking recognition. Such conduct is not merely incorrect; it is rude and disorderly. A call for the question has no effect whatsoever unless a member is properly recognized by the chair, moves the *Previous Question,* and the assembly then adopts the motion to order the *Previous Question* by a two-thirds vote. Many assemblies have the bad habit of permitting a single member or a small minority of members to cut off debate merely by "calling for the question." Do not do it or permit it to be done to you.

Lay on the Table

Purpose and Description. The motion to *Lay on the Table* enables an assembly to temporarily set aside pending business until something more urgent has been taken care of. For example, if a convention business session ran over into the time allotted for a special speaker, the pending business could be laid on the table to accommodate the assembly's wish to hear the speaker.

A question laid on the table is set aside until the assembly votes to resume consideration of it. It may be taken from the table later during the same meeting or convention or at the next regular business meeting.

Lay on the Table is often misused as a means of killing or postponing a main motion. This is an abuse of the motion because *Lay on the Table* is not debatable. It is only fair that proponents of a motion be allowed to discuss its merits before the majority is allowed to delay or kill the motion. If you want to kill a motion, move to *Postpone Indefinitely*. If you want to delay consideration of a question until some later time, move to *Postpone to a Certain Time*. Those are the motions designed for those purposes, both of which are debatable.

Example.

MEMBER: "I move to lay the question on the table."

Call for the Orders of the Day

Purpose and Description. This motion is a demand that the assembly conform to its agenda. If the chairman fails to follow the agenda or the regular order of business or fails to take up a general or special order when the time for it arrives, a single member acting alone can require the chair to enforce the proper schedule of business by calling for the orders of the day. It requires neither a second nor a vote. If the *Call for the Orders of the Day* is in order, the chair and the assembly must comply with the member's demand, unless by a two-thirds vote they choose to set aside the orders of the day and proceed with some other business.

Example.

MEMBER: "I call for the orders of the day."

Question of Privilege

Purpose and Description. A *Question of Privilege* is any matter relating to the rights and privileges of the assembly or of its members that, because of its urgency, must be considered immediately. It generally relates to the comfort, safety, or integrity of members. For example, a problem with the heating, cooling, or lighting of the room could be brought to the chair's attention by raising a

Question of Privilege, as could a problem with the public address system or a disturbance in the meeting hall. A member could correct an inaccurate statement about himself or some other matter concerning his reputation or rights as a member of the body through a *Question of Privilege.*

The motion is usually made in the form of a request to the presiding officer, which he grants or denies. Occasionally, it is made in the form of a motion, which the chair rules is or is not a legitimate *Question of Privilege.* As with all other rulings of the chair, his decisions on handling questions of privilege may be appealed.

The motion is often abused as a guise for debating an issue. The chair should rule the motion out of order when so used. The chair should be firm in admitting as questions of privilege only those matters that relate to the comfort, safety, and integrity of members, and even then he should allow the assembly's business to be interrupted only when the question demands immediate action.

Example.

MEMBER: "I rise to a question of privilege."

CHAIR: "The member will state his question of privilege."

MEMBER: "Mr. Chairman, we cannot hear the speakers over the noise from the exhibit area. May we have the doors at the rear of the hall closed."

CHAIR: "Will the ushers please close the doors at the rear of the hall."

Recess

Purpose and Description. Adopting a motion to *Recess* provides an assembly with a short intermission in their proceedings. While the motion to *Adjourn* terminates a meeting, the motion to *Recess* suspends it for a specified time.

Examples.

> MEMBER: "I move that we recess for fifteen minutes."
>
> Or,
>
> "I move that we recess until eleven o'clock."

Adjourn

Purpose and Description. Adopting the motion to *Adjourn* orders the presiding officer to close the meeting. The reason for the motion's high precedence is that no one should be able to keep a majority of an assembly in session any longer than they want to be. Anytime a majority of members wishes, they can vote to adjourn and go home.

The motion to *Adjourn* is a privileged motion with high precedence except in three cases:

(1) When the motion is qualified in any way, as in a motion to adjourn at a certain hour;

(2) When a time for adjournment has already been set; or

(3) When an adjournment would dissolve the assembly, as happens at the last meeting of a convention (even when an organization has a convention every year, parliamentary law views each convention as a separate body).

In any of these three cases, the motion to *Adjourn* is an incidental main motion and is treated like any other main motion.

Examples.

> MEMBER: "I move that we adjourn."

Or,
"I move that we adjourn at ten o'clock."

In the last example, because the motion to *Adjourn* is qualified, it is not privileged, but is a main motion. It could be made only when no other motion is pending and would be both debatable and amendable.

Fix the Time to Which to Adjourn

Purpose and Description. The hour is late. Members are tired. Some have other appointments for which they are already late. The assembly is about to adjourn, but there is important business on the uncompleted agenda that should be taken up before the next regular business session. What can you do? Move to *Fix the Time to Which to Adjourn.*

This motion enables members to set a time for another meeting to continue the business of the present session. This continuation of the present business session is called an *adjourned meeting.* Anything that could have legally been done at the first meeting can be done at the adjourned meeting. Both meetings together constitute a single *session.* See also the section on *Types of Meetings* in Chapter 5.

Example.

MEMBER: "I move that when we adjourn, we stand adjourned to meet at eight o'clock tomorrow evening."

Point of Order

Purpose and Description. Though the presiding officer is responsible for keeping order in a meeting, occasionally he may fail to notice and correct an error in procedure or a violation of the rules. When that happens, any member may call attention to the error by raising a *Point of Order*.

You do not need to be recognized to raise a *Point of Order*, nor do you need a second. Since a *Point of Order* must be made at the time the breech of order occurs, you may interrupt a speaker to make it.

As soon as you raise a *Point of Order*, the chairman must rule that the point is "well taken" or "not well taken." If the chair rules the point well taken, he orders the error corrected. If he rules it not well taken, he should offer a brief explanation for his ruling, then resume business at the point where it was interrupted.

If the chair rules your point not well taken, you may appeal his decision, in which case the assembly will decide either to sustain or overrule the decision of the chair.

One caution: Do not bother raising a *Point of Order* over every minor irregularity in a meeting. You will only make a nuisance of yourself. Hold out until there is a substantial breech of the rules that violates some right you wish to exercise or prevents the proper transaction of business.

Example.

MEMBER: "I rise to a point of order."
                                Or,
                 "Point of order!"

CHAIR: "The member will state his point of order."

MEMBER: "Mr. Chairman, the speaker who was just assigned the floor has already spoken on the motion and I have not."

CHAIR: "The point of order is well taken. The speaker will please take his seat. The chair recognizes the gentleman who has not yet spoken."

Or,
"The point of order is not well taken. The
member just recognized spoke on the last
motion, but has not yet spoken on the
pending question."

If the chair is in doubt as to how to rule on a *Point of
Order,* he may consult the parliamentarian before render-
ing a decision or he may submit the question to the assembly as follows:

CHAIR: "Mr. A raises a point of order that _____.
The chair is in doubt and submits the question to the assembly. The question is _____."

Appeal

Purpose and Description. Whenever the presiding officer makes a ruling you believe to be mistaken or unfair,
you may appeal to the assembly to reverse the ruling of the
chair. The motion to *Appeal* can be applied only to the rulings of the chair. A statement of fact or an opinion is not
subject to appeal.

Appeals must be made immediately after the chair has
given his ruling. If any business intervenes, it is too late.
Because promptness is important, you do not need to be
recognized by the chair to make an *Appeal,* and you may
interrupt another member if he has been assigned the
floor.

After another member has seconded your *Appeal,* the
chair is allowed to state the reasons for his ruling. *Appeals*
are debatable when they relate to a debatable motion.
When an *Appeal* is debatable, each member may speak
once in debate. The presiding officer is the only member
who may speak twice, once at the beginning and once at

the end of debate. Even when the *Appeal* is not debatable, the chair is allowed to state his reasons for his ruling.

Example.

MEMBER: "I appeal from the decision of the Chair."
          (Second.)

CHAIR: *(After stating the exact question at issue and the reasons for his decision, the chair then states the question on the appeal as follows:)* "The question is: Shall the decision of the chair be sustained?"

                            (Debate)

CHAIR: "As many as are in favor of sustaining the decision of the chair, say aye. . . . Those opposed to sustaining this decision, say no. . . . The ayes (noes) have it and the decision of the chair is sustained (not sustained)."

Note that the question is not on sustaining the chair but on sustaining the decision or ruling of the chair.

Parliamentary Inquiry

Purpose and Description. One of your fundamental rights as a member of an assembly is the right to know what's going on. Are you confused about what the immediately pending question is? Do you want to know the effect of a motion? Are you unsure if a certain motion would be in order? You may ask any procedural question relating to pending business by directing a *Parliamentary Inquiry* to the presiding officer. It is the chairman's duty to assist members in understanding what is going on.

Example.

MEMBER: "Mr. Chairman, I rise to a parliamentary inquiry."

CHAIR: "State your inquiry."

MEMBER: "What motions are now pending?"

CHAIR: "A main motion to adopt the budget, an amendment to line five, and a motion to refer the budget to the finance committee are all pending. The motion to refer is the immediately pending question."

Point of Information

Purpose and Description. A *Point of Information* is a factual question about the business at hand. It is handled like a *Parliamentary Inquiry,* the difference being that it deals with a question of fact and not of parliamentary procedure. A *Point of Information* is directed to the chair or, through the chair, to another member or officer.

Examples.

MEMBER: "Mr. Chairman, I rise to a point of information."

CHAIR: "The member will state his question."

MEMBER: "How long has an annual gift to the American Bible Society been in our missions budget?"

CHAIR: "Will the Treasurer respond to the question?"

Since members are not allowed to speak directly to one another during debate, if you wish to ask a question of a member who is speaking, you must direct your question through the chair. The form is:

MEMBER: "Mr. Chairman, will the speaker yield for a question?"

The speaker may or may not consent to the interruption. If he consents, the time consumed in asking and answering the question is taken out of his allotted time.

Division of the Assembly

Purpose and Description. Any member who doubts the result of a voice vote can call for a *Division of the Assembly,* which requires the chairman to take a rising vote. This demand does not require a second or a vote. It may be made by a single member.

Example.

MEMBER: "I call for a division of the assembly."
Or,
"Division."
CHAIR: "A division is called for. Those in favor of the motion will stand. . . ."

Division of a Question

Purpose and Description. The motion *Division of a Question* enables an assembly to divide a pending main motion that is composed of several independent parts. The assembly then separately considers and votes upon the individual motions into which the question has been divided.

In most cases, the motion to divide a question requires a second and a majority vote. The exception is when a series of independent resolutions or motions dealing with different subjects is offered as a single motion. In that case a single member may demand a separate vote on any or all of the resolutions or motions offered in block.

Examples. Suppose the chair has just stated the following question: "That the church receive a special Christmas Offering for Christian City Children's Home and that we add them to this year's missions budget." If you wanted to separately consider those two proposals, you would say:

> MEMBER: "Mr. Chairman, I move to divide the question so that the question of adding Christian City Children's Home to this year's missions budget be considered separately."

Convention committees often move the adoption of a group of resolutions in block. If you want to single out a particular resolution for discussion and a vote, say:

> MEMBER: "Mr. Chairman, I call for a separate vote on Resolution Number Six."

Suspend the Rules

Purpose and Description. Occasionally, an assembly needs to do something that would violate its regular rules of procedure. The assembly may take the action by adopting a motion to *Suspend the Rules.*

Only procedural rules may be suspended. Bylaws may not be suspended. Rules that protect the rights of individual members or of absentees may not be suspended. When making the motion, you must say exactly what action you wish to take. If adopted, the motion suspends only the particular rule that prevents the specific action you proposed.

A two-thirds vote is usually required to suspend a rule. Noncontroversial matters involving the suspension of rules can frequently be carried out by unanimous consent.

In conventions the motion is most often used to take up items of business out of their fixed order in the agenda.

Example.

MEMBER: "Mr. Chairman, I move to suspend the rules and proceed to take up the report of the Evangelism Committee."

Reconsider

Purpose and Description. Assemblies do make mistakes. The motion to *Reconsider* enables an assembly to bring back for further consideration a motion that has already been voted on. If adopted, the original motion comes back before the meeting as if it had never been voted on.

Only a member who voted on the prevailing side can make a motion to *Reconsider.* A motion may be reconsidered only in the same session in which it was adopted. In business sessions of more than one day, such as a convention, a motion can be reconsidered on the day it was made or on the following day.

Reconsider is the only motion with a split order of precedence for its making and its consideration. The motion may be *made* and seconded at any time and takes precedence over any other motion that is pending. The member who makes the motion to *Reconsider* can even interrupt another member who has been assigned the floor if he has not yet begun to speak. But with respect to its *consideration,* the motion to *Reconsider* has only the same rank as the motion to be reconsidered. For example, if you wanted to reconsider a main motion that had been adopted earlier in a meeting, you could move to reconsider the motion anytime, even if the assembly was already considering other business. But your motion to *Reconsider* could be stated to the assembly and discussed only at a time when a main motion would be in order.

The motion to *Reconsider* is debatable when the motion to which it is applied is debatable. It is one of the exceptions to the rule that members can debate only the immediately pending question. Debate on a motion to *Reconsider* may also go into the merits of the motion to which it is applied.

Usually only main motions are reconsidered.

Examples.

MEMBER: "I move to reconsider the vote on the motion to invite Dr. Lorraine Chesnut to be our revival speaker."

If consideration of a motion to *Reconsider* is not in order when it is made, the chair says:

CHAIR: "The secretary will note that it is moved and seconded to reconsider the vote on the motion to invite Dr. Chesnut to be our revival speaker."

When the time comes that the motion to *Reconsider* can be considered, the maker of the motion obtains the floor and proceeds:

MEMBER: "I call up the motion to reconsider the vote on the motion to invite Dr. Lorraine Chesnut to be our revival speaker."

CHAIR: "The motion to reconsider the vote on the motion to invite Dr. Lorraine Chesnut to be our revival speaker is called up. The question is on the motion to reconsider. Is there any discussion?"

When the chair puts the motion to a vote, he should be clear that the members understand that they are not yet voting again on the original motion, but only on whether they are going to reconsider it. The chair should announce the result of the vote as follows:

> CHAIR: "The ayes have it and the motion to reconsider is carried. The question is now on the motion to invite Dr. Chesnut to be our revival speaker."
>
> Or,
>
> "The noes have it and the motion to invite Dr. Chesnut to be our next revival speaker will not be reconsidered."

In effect, it takes two votes to complete the reconsideration of a question. An affirmative vote on the motion to *Reconsider,* then a second vote on the original motion.

There is a special form of this motion called *Reconsider and Enter on the Minutes.* It can be made only on the same day the motion to be reconsidered was voted upon, and it cannot be called up until another day. It can be applied only to votes that finally dispose of a main motion. The purpose of the motion is to prevent a temporary majority from taking advantage of a low turnout at a meeting. If moved and seconded, *Reconsider and Enter on the Minutes* suspends action on the motion it is applied to until the next meeting of the assembly. In effect, it permits any two members to temporarily block action on a main motion. Since the motion could easily be abused, it should be used only in extreme cases when an unrepresentative majority attempts to take an action that would be opposed by a majority of the membership. The form for making the motion is:

> MEMBER: "I move to reconsider and enter on the minutes the vote on the motion to _____."

Rescind or Amend Something Previously Adopted

Purpose and Description. Rescind and *Amend Something Previously Adopted* are two forms of the same motion. Whereas the motion to *Reconsider* can undo an action previously taken in the same business session, the motions to *Rescind* or to *Amend Something Previously Adopted* can change the text of or strike out an entire motion no matter how long ago it was passed.

Debate on both motions may go into the merits of the motion to which they are applied, since the substance of the matter to be rescinded or amended is certainly germane to the decision to rescind or amend.

If a motion has been carried out, it cannot be rescinded or amended. If it has been partially carried out, only the unexecuted part can be rescinded or amended.

In order to protect members who may be absent from a regular meeting, the motions to *Rescind* or to *Amend Something Previously Adopted* require more than a simple majority vote. Either motion can be adopted by: (1) A two-thirds vote; (2) a majority vote if previous notice was given at the last regular meeting or in the call of the present meeting; or (3) a majority vote of the entire membership.

Examples.

MEMBER: "I move to rescind the motion 'That the church cancel evening worship during the summer months,' which was adopted at the April meeting."

Or,

"In accordance with notice given at the last meeting, I move to rescind the motion 'That the church cancel evening worship during the summer months,' which was adopted at the April meeting."

Take From the Table

Purpose and Description. Take From the Table brings back any motion previously laid on the table. A motion laid on the table may be taken from the table during same or during the next regular meeting. When consideration of a tabled motion is resumed, it returns to the assembly exactly as it was when laid on the table.

Example.

MEMBER: "I move to take from the table the motion relating to our fall revival."

Summary

These 23 motions are the fundamental tools of the deliberative assembly. Learn each motion's purpose, its classification, its order of precedence, the basic rules governing its use, and the form for making it. The chart on *Rules and Precedence of Motions* in the front of this book is especially important. Most of what you need to know about the system of motions is on that chart. Study it carefully and keep it with you in your meetings.

4
Debate

Roger Sherman, signer of the Declaration of Independence and member of the Constitutional Convention of 1787, is said to have summed up his parliamentary strategy with this advise: "When you are in a minority, talk; when you are in a majority, vote."[1]

Talking and voting are the two most important elements of the parliamentary process. All the rules and technicalities are directed toward helping members discuss issues and make decisions. This chapter will explain how to organize and present your ideas in a parliamentary speech and how to use some basic strategy to adopt or defeat motions.

How to Give a Parliamentary Speech

1. Say Clearly, Concisely, and Immediately Why You Wish to Have the Floor.

Parliamentary speeches are too short to waste time waiting for the chairman or the members to figure out what you are up to. Do not keep them guessing. Tell them immediately why you have taken the floor.

If you support the pending motion, say:

MEMBER: "Mr. Chairman, I rise to speak in favor of the motion because . . . ."

If you want to defeat the motion, say:

> MEMBER: "Mr. Chairman, I am opposed to this motion because. . . ."

If you wish to amend, postpone, refer, or move some other subsidiary or incidental action on the motion, say so plainly. Use the *exact parliamentary language* for whatever you want the chair or the assembly to do. For example:

> MEMBER: "Mr. Chairman, I move to amend the motion by striking the word 'twenty-five' and inserting the word 'ten'."
>
> Or,
>
> MEMBER: "Mr. Chairman, I move to refer the motion to a special committee of three consisting of Mr. Woolard, Mr. Pressley, and Mrs. Lewis, with instructions to report at the next regular meeting."

Do not make the chair or the assembly guess whether you are asking a question, making a request, or debating the question:

> MEMBER: "Mr. Chairman, I rise to a parliamentary inquiry. If adopted, what would be the effect of the pending motion?"
>
> Or,
>
> MEMBER: "Mr. Chairman, I rise to a point of order. The motion just proposed is out of order because the bylaws forbid the church's endorsing a political candidate."
>
> Or,
>
> MEMBER: "Mr. Chairman, I favor the motion because. . . ."

Use the exact parliamentary language for whatever action you want to take. People will not be persuaded to do what you want to have done until they understand what you want to have done. By using the exact parliamentary language to state why you have taken the floor, you make yourself immediately understood.

2. Make One Simple, Bold Point to Support Your Position on the Pending Question.

First, choose one specific reason you are for or against the pending motion. Why? In most cases you will be only one of several speakers who debate the motion. Under the regular rules you have a maximum of ten minutes to make your case. A limitation on debate would give you even less time. Remember, too, that the number of speakers, the time already spent in debate, the temperature of the room, how close you are to lunch, and a dozen other things can shorten your audience's attention span. You may have several good reasons for your position. But so do the other speakers with whom you must share the floor. To win the vote on the motion, you must compel the members not only to believe your speech, but to remember it when the vote is taken.

Given these limitations, you have a better chance of persuading the audience with one clear, concise, unforgettable reason to vote with you on the motion. If, after you have spoken once, you need further reasons to persuade the audience, seek the floor again. But each time you rise to speak, focus your thoughts on a single relevant reason for the motion that addresses the exact issue under discussion at the moment you take the floor.

Follow this rule, and your fellow members will catch on that you are no floor hog. Other speakers may drone on and on with a dozen points on every issue; when you rise to speak, you want the people to hear one clear, concise, persuasive reason to vote your way on the motion. If you need the floor again to rebut opponents or to offer additional support for your proposal, the people will not mind giving you leave to speak.

Next, condense the specific reason for your position into one simple, bold point. Good speeches have a thesis, a single sentence that states as precisely and vividly as possible the reason for adopting or rejecting the motion. This one, simple, bold point is the thumb-tack with which you pin your speech to your listener's mental bulletin board. It must be short, simple, and sharp enough to persuade and to be remembered.

Finally, get to the point at the beginning of your speech. Just as parliamentary speeches are too short for you to waste time waiting for the chair or the members to figure out exactly *what* you want to do, so they are also too short for you to keep the members guessing about *why* you want to do it. The members are not interested in watching you buzz the field. They want to know where you are going to land. Do not keep them waiting. Get to the point of the motion. As soon as you have the floor, state your thesis.

3. Prove Your Point.

Four centuries before Christ, Aristotle figured out that there were two indispensible parts of a speech. First you must state your case, he said, and then you must prove it. His advice still applies. You distilled the best reason for your position into a single, vivid sentence, your thesis. You opened your speech with that thesis. Your task now is to prove, to explain, or to apply that thesis to the question at hand. Give your listeners enough relevant facts to carry your point.

Examples, analogies, statistics (if they are simple and well visualized), definitions, quotations (if they are short and used sparingly), and visual aids (slides, maps, graphs) can be marshalled in support of your position.

Tell your listeners who, what, where, when, why, and how. Give them specific facts and details that will convince them to vote with you on the motion.

For example, do you want your church to spend more to send Bibles to the mission field? When you rise to speak for the motion, tell them a story to prove your point:

MEMBER: "When Leslie Weatherhead was five years old he bought a Bible from a preacher for a penny. He wrote his name in the flyleaf and sent the Bible to a missionary in India. At an evangelistic meeting the missionary gave the Bible to a native from a remote village. Twenty years later, when other missionaries reached that distant region, they found a fully functioning church. The native had proclaimed the gospel, converted his people, and organized a church with no other guide than a penny Bible given by a five-year-old boy half a world away. Were the souls of those people worth the boy's penny? Then this motion to send more Bibles to the mission field is worth our money as well!"

4. Restate Your Thesis and Call for Action.

You have proved your point. Your listeners liked what you had to say. They are convinced you are right. Now, make sure they know what to do about it.

This part of your speech will take at most fifteen seconds. But it is this crucial point in a parliamentary speech where all could be won or lost. In your introduction you told your listeners the most compelling reason for your position in your thesis sentence. Once you have proved your point, repeat the thesis, then ask the assembly to adopt or reject the motion. Do not assume they will know what to do. You tell them.

> MEMBER: "Mr. Chairman, fools rush in where angels fear to tread. Let's not be fools. I urge the assembly to adopt the motion to refer."

Or,

> MEMBER: "The motion before us is to amend the budget by allocating $543 to send 100 Bibles to the mission field. But the real question is this: Is a human soul worth $5.43? I think so. I urge the assembly to adopt the amendment."

All your eloquence counts for nothing if your listeners do not know whether to stand with the ayes or the noes when the vote is taken. Be sure that your final sentence pins a note to your listeners' minds that says "Vote yes" or "Vote no."

Basic Parliamentary Strategy

When you read what I have written about parliamentary strategy, I do not want you to think that church meetings should be some sort of competitive arenas where the side with the superior skills in gamesmanship is always the victor. Parliamentary procedure is not a bag of tricks for winning on technicalities what you cannot win on substance. The rules exist to enable an assembly of people,

Christian brothers and sisters in this case, to fairly and efficiently conduct their business. Use the rules to exercise your rights as a member. Use them to present and defend your ideas in the best possible fashion. Use them to oppose motions you believe the assembly should reject. But do not be negative, obstructive, or partisan about it.

Now, how do you win the assembly's acceptance of your ideas? To begin with, the fundamental key to success in persuading your fellow members to see things your way in a meeting is: *Be prepared!*

In his autobiography, Air Force General Chuck Yeager, the first man to fly faster than the speed of sound, explained that a test pilot stays alive by learning the emergency systems, asking questions of the engineers, and studying the pilot's handbook for every airplane he flies. Otherwise excellent pilots who are not interested in doing that kind of homework often wind up dead.

Yeager said that thorough preparation saved his life in 1947 during one of the test flights of the Bell X-1. Just as Yeager's experimental aircraft was dropped from the belly of a B-29 at 25,000 feet, all of the electrical controls and switches, including his rocket ignition, went dead. Without power, he could still glide, but loaded with over 600 gallons of fuel the X-1 would fall too fast to land safely. Even the electrical switch that controlled the propellant valve to jettison his fuel was dead. The position of the X-1's razor-sharp wings made bailing out impossible. Yeager found himself riding a 13,000 pound bomb to the ground.

Nevertheless, Yeager lived to tell the story of that flight because he and the X-1's engineer, Dick Frost, had prepared for just such a total power failure. Before the first X-1 flights, Frost bought a $25 valve, which he attached to a bottle of nitrogen gas in the cockpit. This crude emergency jettison system enabled Yeager to expel his fuel in the air and glide to a safe landing.

Though speaking up in a meeting is not as dangerous an enterprise as flying experimental aircraft, Yeager's method of staying alive is the same for keeping your ideas and motions alive in a parliamentary assembly: Be prepared.

The following suggestions will prepare you to guide your proposals through to adoption by your assembly.

What to Do Before the Meeting

1. Know the Rules.

You cannot exercise rights you do not know you have. You cannot use a rule you do not know exists. Study this book. Study your assembly's parliamentary authority (usually *Robert's Rules of Order Newly Revised*). Gain as much knowledge and experience in parliamentary procedure as you can.

Consider this personal example of how it pays to know the rules. In 1986 I was serving as chairman of the North Carolina Social Services Commission. The commission is a quasi-legislative body appointed by the governor that adopts regulations for administering all social programs in the state. I favored a motion to adopt a controversial and highly publicized regulation concerning the state abortion fund which opponents of the regulation had moved to refer to the legislature, a majority of whom would probably have been unsympathetic to the regulation.

This was a smart move on our opponents' part because the executive and legislative branches of our state government at that time were controlled by opposing political parties. My party held a majority on the commission, but the opponents' party held a majority in the legislature.

After vigorous debate on the motion to *Refer*, one of the six commissioners from my party voted with the other side, giving the motion to *Refer* a five to four majority. To everyone in the room—the commissioners on both sides, the staff, the press, and the public—it looked as if our opponents had won. And they would have had I not known two commonly overlooked rules of parliamentary procedure: A chairman may not only vote to break a tie but may vote to *create* one, and a tie vote is not a deadlock, but a losing vote. I announced the vote on the motion to *Refer* this way:

CHAIR: "There are five in the affirmative and four in the negative. The chair votes in the negative, making five in the affirmative and five in the negative. The affirmative and the negative are tied. The motion to refer is lost. The question is now on the adoption of the regulation. Is there any further discussion?"

The commissioner who had moved to refer the regulation immediately challenged my action, but withdrew his challenge when I pointed out the two rules involved. In the ensuing discussion, one of the commissioners who had voted for the motion to *Refer* was persuaded to support the regulation and it was adopted, five to four without my vote. Though I had not participated in debate on either motion and had, as was my duty as chairman, exercised the strictest impartiality in enforcing the rules during the proceedings, I was able to influence the outcome of the decision because I knew the rules.

2. Get the Facts.

A working knowledge of the rules of procedure will help you get things done in a meeting, but it will not substitute for having something of substance to say when you stand up to speak.

No amount of spit and polish can make up for a lack of factual support for your motion. The best speeches in any forum are undergirded with careful, unhurried study, thought, and research of the subject. A deficit of information will bankrupt your speech. Do not wait until your plane is in the air or you are on the floor of the assembly to discover you do not have the facts you need to do the job. Get them ahead of time.

Get a copy of each meeting's agenda ahead of time, if possible. Get the facts on motions and reports in which you have an interest. Have a copy of your bylaws, rules, and parliamentary authority with you at the meeting.

3. Write Out Your Motion Ahead of Time.

I once had the misfortune of serving on a board of directors with a long-winded man who never thought out or wrote down his motions, but always composed them on his feet. His motions usually became so long and complex that he would himself forget what he had already said in his own motion. Often he had to ask the secretary to read back the first part of his motion before he could complete it. This man could have improved his motions and saved us time if he had only taken the trouble to write them out ahead of time.

Be sure your motion says exactly what you want the assembly to do. Keep a copy for yourself and make a copy to send to the chair when you make the motion. The chairman and the secretary will appreciate the courtesy shown them, and the chairman will have the exact wording of your motion when he states it to the assembly.

4. Have a Respected Seconder for Your Motion and Line up Your Support.

Do not wait until you are in the meeting to see if anyone seconds or speaks for your motion. Line up enthusiastic, articulate supporters ahead of time and brief them on the strong points of your idea. Make sure they attend the meeting and speak out.

Having said that, let me caution you against politicizing church business. A religious assembly is not a political convention. It is not a place for cutting deals and trading favors. It is an opportunity for the people of God to collectively discern the will of God in the matters that concern His kingdom here. Though you may enthusiastically promote your ideas and allow others to the hear the good points of your proposals, never be guilty of turning your religious assembly into a battleground for rival factions to fight it out.

In this chapter the term *opponents* is used to describe members who oppose a particular motion that you support. Never speak of a fellow member of your assembly as *your* opponent or enemy. When brothers and sisters in Christ differ in their opinions and oppose one another's *ideas,* they should do so with kindness and respect.

What to Do During the Meeting

If you have drafted a good motion and have prepared a good speech in its support, just making and explaining your motion may be enough to convince your fellow members to adopt it. Occasionally, though, you will have procedural obstacles to overcome in order for your motion to be adopted. The following suggestions should help you in using the rules to your advantage.

1. Position Your Motion for Favorable Consideration.

Make your motion early in the meeting, before members are tired or other motions have preempted the action you wish to take. Or, make your motion a special order and set it to be considered just after a recess or, in the case of a convention, as the opening item of business at one of the sessions.

There may well be other considerations that come into play in your particular situation. But know this, there *is* a best time to present and discuss your proposal. Figure out when that best time is and try to position your motion in or close to that time slot.

2. Expose Weaknesses in Your Opponents' Arguments by Asking Questions.

Proverbs 18:17 says: "The first to present his case seems right, till another comes forward and questions him."[2] You may raise a *Point of Information* to question an opponent's facts, reasoning, or sources of information. Questions can bring to light facts omitted by an opponent's speech or can draw out points that help your case.

Do not be argumentative when asking questions of a speaker. Do not put him on the defensive. Ask your question in a way that encourages the speaker to supply the information you need. Do not use a *Point of Information* to make a speech yourself. If you want to draw conclusions from the speaker's answers, wait until he has finished, then seek the floor and make your comments.

3. Use Parliamentary Inquiries to Be Sure Your Supporters Know How to Vote on Procedural Questions Affecting Your Motion.

Parliamentary Inquiries are helpful, first, when you really do not know what is going on. But they are also helpful when you do know what is going on, but you are not so sure about the rest of the assembly. Often members who support a main motion will not know how to vote on some procedural question that affects the motion. Make sure the assembly fully realizes the effect that any proposed action will have on your motion. For example, if you believe a majority of the members support your motion, but opponents have moved to refer it to a committee, you could raise a *Parliamentary Inquiry:*

MEMBER: "Mr. Chairman, I rise to a parliamentary inquiry."

CHAIR: "State your inquiry."

MEMBER: "Mr. Chairman, if we adopt the motion to refer, will members of the assembly who support the motion be able to vote to adopt it today?"

CHAIR: "No, the motion would be referred to the committee and the assembly would not be able to act on it again until the committee reports on the motion at our regular meeting next quarter."

MEMBER: "So, if a member wants to adopt the motion today, rather than waiting three months to put it into effect, then he should vote no on the motion to refer?"

CHAIR: "That is correct."

MEMBER: "Thank you, Mr. Chairman."

The question was not for your benefit but to make clear to the members who support your motion that they should vote against referral.

4. Speak and Vote Against Indefinite Postponement.

Remember that *Postpone Indefinitely* has no other purpose than to politely kill the main motion on which it is moved. In most cases, if you are out to win approval for your idea, it makes little difference whether your motion is killed by a direct vote or quietly dies in its sleep by indefinite postponement. It is still dead.

If you are certain the assembly is going to defeat your motion, try to refer it to committee or postpone it to a later meeting. If those measures fail, there could be a slight advantage to having your motion postponed indefinitely. If, when you re-introduce your motion at a later meeting, opponents characterize it as "the motion we defeated last time," you can argue that the motion was not defeated, but merely postponed.

5. Support Any Amendments That Would Strengthen Your Motion; Oppose Any That Would Weaken It.

Another member may offer an amendment that makes your motion better or makes it more palatable to the assembly. Be quick to voice your own support for such amendments. Vigorously oppose any attempts to weaken your motion with adverse amendments.

In fact, if your motion presents a strong position on a controversial issue, it is not a bad idea to prepare admendments or a substitute for your own motion. The substitute could be a more moderate version of your motion that you retreat to if the opposition is strong. Or, the substitute could be a stronger version that you make with the intention of sacrificing it. If they think your original proposal too radical, have someone move the stronger substitute to show the opposition what a really radical motion looks like. After the assembly defeats the radical substitute, your original motion may not look as strong as it did initially, and adopting it may appear to be a reasonable compromise.

6. Speak and Vote Against Attempts to Delay Action on Your Motion.

Generally, delaying tactics work against a motion. So in most cases you should try to avoid having your motion referred, postponed, or laid on the table. But do not be afraid to use these motions if you sense that you are losing ground and need time to rally support.

Under no circumstances should you allow your motion to be *killed* by being laid on the table. Remember that *Lay On the Table* is intended to briefly set aside some pending business so that an urgent, more important matter can be considered first. The motion is out of order when it is used to kill another motion without debate. Unless the member who moves to table your motion can say what urgent business needs to interrupt its consideration, raise a *Point of Order*. If the chairman himself does not realize this is a misuse of *Lay on the Table*—which is possible since this error is so common—then politely refer him to the section covering the motion in *Robert's Rules of Order Newly Revised*.

If opponents seek to postpone your motion, move to amend their motion to *Postpone* so that your motion receives the best possible positioning. Move to postpone your own motion if you sense that you don't have the votes to adopt it right now.

Amend any motions to refer your motion to a hostile committee by substituting a friendly committee. If I thought a favorable committee report on my motion would improve its chances of adoption, I would try to refer it myself.

7. Use the Previous Question to Your Advantage.

If you sense that the majority is behind your motion and that they are ready to vote, move the *Previous Question*.

Vote against the *Previous Question* if you need time to gain support. Try to bring your motion to a vote as soon as you think it has won the assembly's support.

Be careful, though, of being too quick in cutting off members who want to speak against a motion. To be fair, you need to give the opposition a chance to state their case. For one thing, they just might be right! Even if not, you do not want to appear to be railroading your motion through the meeting. But once it seems clear that a vocal minority is holding up a vote, do not hesitate to move the *Previous Question.*

8. Use the Motion to Recess to Your Advantage.

Move to *Recess* if you think you need time to caucus with your motion's supporters. Vote against *Recess* if it would break your momentum and allow opponents of your motion to regroup.

Recesses are another good tool to use when you are not sure that supporters of your motion know which way to vote on some procedural motion that is essential to getting to and passing the main motion. A recess can bring a break in the action to allow you to caucus with supporters.

You may also use a recess to speak privately to opponents of your motion. Often you may come to an understanding that leads to their acceptance of your proposal or to amendments that would make your motion acceptable to all concerned.

9. Once Adopted, See That Your Motion Is Carried Out Immediately.

Any motion can be rescinded or amended after its passage, unless it has already been carried out. Once your motion becomes the will of the assembly, see that it is carried out immediately.

Be sure that your motion specifies which officer, committee, or agency of the assembly is responsible for carrying out your motion. Do not be like the church that had an important job to be done but did not say who was supposed to do it. Everybody was sure that Somebody would do it. Anybody could have done it, but Nobody did it. When Everybody found out that Nobody had done the job, Everybody was angry because it was Somebody's job. So it ended up that Everybody blamed Somebody because Nobody did the job that Anybody could have done in the first place. Make sure your motion names the somebody who is supposed to do whatever action your motion orders.

10. Be Sure the Minutes of the Meeting Fully and Accurately Record the Assembly's Action on Your Motion.

Pay close attention to the reading and approval of the minutes at the meeting after your motion was adopted. Be sure they say exactly what the assembly did with your motion. The minutes are the official, legal record of the assembly's proceedings. If there are any future questions about your motion, the minutes are the place the assembly or—God forbid, but it does happen—the courts will look for answers. If your motion is not in the minutes, it did not happen!

Though an inaccurate set of minutes can be later corrected by a motion to *Amend Something Previously Adopted,* it is a lot easier to correct any errors at the time the minutes are actually approved.

11. If Your Motion Is Lost, Move to Reconsider or Renew It at a Future Meeting.

A motion may be reconsidered later in the same meeting. After that, the motion may be re-introduced as a new motion at any subsequent meeting of the assembly.

You may not move to *Reconsider* a motion unless you voted on the prevailing side. If a motion you supported failed, you must ask the assembly's permission to change your vote before you can move to *Reconsider*. Or, you can persuade someone who voted against your motion make the motion to *Reconsider*.

How to Defeat a Motion

No one likes an obstructionist or a naysayer. But making good decisions involves both adopting good motions and rejecting bad ones. If you believe the adoption of a motion would be bad for the assembly, you should oppose it.

Prepare yourself as well as you can for action against the motion. Know the rules. Get the facts on why the motion you oppose should be rejected. Have respected members of the assembly join you in speaking and voting against it.

Once in the meeting you may legitimately take any of the following actions to attempt the motion's defeat. Most of these are mirror images of the various stratagems for adopting motions.

1. Speak Against the Motion.

Allow the maker of the motion the courtesy and right to speak first in favor of his motion. But seek to be recognized as quickly as you can after he yields the floor and speak against the motion. Be gracious and positive, and make sure your remarks are directed against the measure and not the man who made it. If you believe the motion is a bad idea, say so as plainly and forcefully as you can. Follow the same steps detailed at the beginning of the chapter for making your speech.

2. Vote Against the Motion.

I list speaking and voting against the motion first because they are the most straightforward methods of expressing your opposition to any proposal. They are also fundamental rights of every member. No one can fault you for honestly speaking your mind or voting as your conscience dictates. You have the right to vote no, even if you are the only member to do so.

3. Expose Weakness in Arguments Offered by the Motion's Supporters.

If the motion would have undesirable consequences, bring those to light by making a *Parliamentary Inquiry* of the chair. If you detect a weakness in a speaker's arguments, ask if he will yield for a question or later raise a *Point of Information* to bring out facts which the motion's supporters may have missed.

4. Move to Postpone Indefinitely.

Moving to *Postpone Indefinitely* doubles your opportunity to speak and vote against the pending question. A member who has exhausted his right to speak on the main motion can speak again on the motion to *Postpone Indefinitely*. You also have the chance to gage the strength of the main motion by watching the vote on indefinite postponement.

5. Move to Amend the Motion

The best use of the motion to *Amend* is to propose changes to an objectionable motion so that, if amended, you can then support it. Amendments can be great tools for bringing opposing sides together to support an amended motion that is pleasing to both.

Another, though less positive, amending tactic is to encumber the motion with adverse amendments that make it unacceptable to the majority and thereby increase the probability of its defeat. Though often done in legislative bodies, this tactic is dangerous. If the amendment carries, you run the risk of then helping to adopt a really terrible motion.

6. Move to Delay Consideration of the Motion.

The first reason to delay a motion is to provide time to improve it, if that is possible. A committee can study the question and offer amendments or a substitute motion. A postponement can give members time to think about the question and come up with alternatives. Many motions that would be adopted in the heat of the moment are found to be defective when given second thought.

If you believe an action to be hasty or unstudied, say so. Remind the assembly that, if after thinking upon the question they still want to adopt it, they can always do so when the motion comes up again for consideration.

7. Use the Previous Question to Your Advantage.

If a motion has had a fair hearing and the assembly appears to be against it, move the *Previous Question* to bring it to a vote. If, on the other hand, you believe an immediate vote will result in the hasty adoption of a bad motion, vote against ordering the *Previous Question*.

Because the *Previous Question* is not debatable, if you oppose an immediate vote, you cannot speak against it. You could, however, give notice that if the *Previous Question* is defeated you will move some other subsidiary motion. For example:

MEMBER: "Mr. Chairman, since I believe the pending question needs additional study before its adoption, I wish to give notice that if the motion to order the previous question fails, I will move to refer the pending question to the Missions Committee."

Since, technically, the member is not debating the previous question, but is giving notice of his intention to make a motion, his comments are in order.

8. Use the Motion to Recess to Your Advantage.

A motion to *Recess* can give you time to caucus with fellow opponents of the motion or it can break the momentum of the other side. If you are close to what you think will be a negative vote on the motion, try to block any delays by voting against a motion to *Recess* or amending it to set the recess for a later time.

9. Move to Adjourn.

One of the simplest and most effective ways to kill an item of business is to adjourn the meeting while it is under consideration or before reaching that point in the agenda. If the hour is late and the members tired, your motion to *Adjourn* is likely to have a favorable reception.

10. Raise a Point of No Quorum If You Doubt the Presence of a Quorum.

A presiding officer or a member who notices the absence of a quorum and remains silent has failed to do his duty. If, at the same time, he also allows his opponents to conduct business that is to their advantage, he is being foolish as well. Remember that a quorum is assumed to be present until it is proven otherwise. If you doubt the presence of a quorum, say something. The procedure for raising a point of no quorum is discussed in the section on *Quorum of Members* in Chapter 5.

I once watched the opponents of a controversial bylaws revision for a state assembly defeat it by delaying action on the proposed revision until the afternoon of the last day of a convention. They continued debate on the issue until enough delegates had gone home, then raised a point of no quorum. When the chair counted, there was slightly less than a quorum of delegates present. He had no choice but to declare the convention adjourned and the objectionable revision of the bylaws died with the final rap of the gavel.

11. If the Motion Passes, Move to Reconsider or to Rescind.

Opponents and proponents alike have the right to ask the assembly to change its mind. If you are in the same business session, try to *Reconsider*. If in a later session, try to *Rescind*.

If you believe that an unrepresentatively small majority has taken advantage of a low turnout at a meeting to take an action that a majority of the membership is opposed to, then move to *Reconsider and Enter on the Minutes*. If another member will join you in seconding the motion, the two of you alone can delay final action on a main motion until a later meeting, to which you could rally the members to express the will of an actual majority of the assembly.

What to Do If You Lose

As a member of a deliberative assembly, you may in good conscience use every legitimate parliamentary tactic in the book to adopt motions you support and to defeat motions you oppose. But once you have exhausted all avenues open to you under the rules or when you believe further opposition will be useless, quit. It is time to yield to the will of the majority.

No member in a meeting has the right to speak adversely of any prior act of the assembly unless he is making, speaking, or giving notice of a motion to *Reconsider, Rescind,* or *Amend Something Previously Adopted*. If the majority of the assembly has clearly asserted their will on a matter, it is time for you to graciously accept their will, or at least be quiet. If an assembly to which you belong takes an action that so violates your conscience that you can no longer bear to be associated with it, then resign. But do not be a murmurer or backbiter. Do not sow seeds of dissention within your own body. It will profit neither you nor your assembly.

While in graduate school, the congregation to which I belonged nominated a slate of candidates to serve as elders of the church. One of the men on the slate had recently been irregular in attending worship services. He was not even present that day as we were voting on his election as an elder. His nomination bothered me, especially since this kind of bad decision was uncharacteristic of the doctrinal soundness that usually distinguished the congregation. When the slate was proposed, I asked why his name was on the ballot. Various members and officers of the church nervously offered excuses for his infrequent attendance. What it boiled down to was that he was a prominent man in the community, had given a lot of money to the church, and had helped the church in doing business with the bank of which he was a vice-president. I expressed my gratitude for all the man's help but insisted that his forsaking the assembling of the saints made him spiritually unfit to be a bishop over God's people. Though I sensed that a number of other members felt as I did, this was the first time a dissenting voice had ever been raised in a church election, and they failed to speak up. I lost a motion to amend the slate by deleting this man's name, but my arguments apparently had some effect since a voice vote to adopt the slate of nominees brought only several weak ayes from around the church. Still, I was the only member to vote no on the motion, and it carried.

After the meeting I approached the elders of the church to say that I still believed the decision to be wrong but that I had voiced my opposition in the meeting, the congregation had spoken on the matter, and I would abide by their decision. My conciliatory response after the meeeting had two positive effects. It enhanced my reputation as a loyal member of the congregation who would speak his mind but who would gracefully yield to the will of the church. It also eventually led to the repentance and reformation of the man I had opposed and in the church's taking a more serious approach to electing men to church office.

Do not be guilty of mutiny. Do everything the rules allow to oppose proposals you believe should be defeated. Do everything the rules allow to support proposals you believe should be adopted. But when it's all over, gracefully yield to the will of the majority.

Decorum in Debate

The customs and formalities of parliamentary debate exist largely to help members maintain their decorum while discussing issues. You may attack an idea or a motion made in a meeting, but you must never attack another member. The motion, not the person who made it, should always be the point at issue. This is the reason that all remarks in debate should be directed to the chair, not to other members.

Both Scripture and parliamentary law forbid the abuse or slander of a person in a meeting. Under the rules, no speaker may use language that:

1. Reflects on another member's conduct or character.
2. Is discourteous or unnecessarily harsh.
3. Attacks or questions a member's motives.

4. Implies the truth of rumors, contains insinuations, or makes allegations against another member's good name.

The moment the chair hears such words used about a member in debate or in a motion he must act immediately to correct the matter and prevent its repetition.

The chair may choose to first warn the speaker by rapping the gavel lightly, pointing out the fault, and advising the member to avoid it. If the breach continues, the chair calls the member to order as follows:

CHAIR: "The member is out of order and will be seated."

If the member apologizes or withdraws his remarks, the chair can put this question (which is undebatable) to the assembly:

CHAIR: "Shall the member be allowed to continue speaking? As many as are in favor, say 'aye'. . . ."

The rules do not forbid you from making legitimate charges against a member whom you believe has committed a serious offense for which he ought to be disciplined. But they do require that accusations against a member be made through a fair disciplinary process, all of which should be conducted in executive session. Be as careful of another member's reputation as you would your own.

NOTES

1. Roger Sherman, as cited by Catherine Drinker Bowen, *Miracle at Philadelphia* (Boston: Little, Brown and Co., 1966), p. 93.

2. From the HOLY BIBLE *New International Version*, copyright © 1978, New York Bible Society. Used by permission.

5
Meetings

A deliberative assembly can act only in a duly called meeting of its members. No officer, member, or group of members may act on behalf of the assembly without an official meeting to discuss and adopt a motion or rule authorizing that action. The decision-making powers of the group must be exercised collectively.

Meetings are the official gatherings of the members of a deliberative body to conduct business. If an assembly holds a series of meetings to conduct a single agenda over several days, such as in a convention, each separate gathering of members is called a *meeting* and the series of meetings is called a *session*.

Types of Meetings

Regular meetings are the stated periodic business sessions of a permanent organization. Your church or organization's bylaws should state when regular meetings are held.

An assembly may also call *special meetings* to handle urgent business that cannot wait for a regular meeting. Special meetings are *called* by giving notice of the time, place, and purpose of the meeting to every member of the assembly. The notice of a special meeting is referred to as the *call of the meeting*. Your bylaws should say who may call special meetings and how notice shall be given to members. Only those items of business mentioned in the call of the meeting may be acted upon at a special meeting. Nothing else may be considered.

An *adjourned meeting* is a continuation of another meeting. Any meeting can be adjourned to a further time by adopting a motion to *Fix the Time to Which to Adjourn*. An adjourned meeting continues the agenda of the previous meeting at whatever point it was interrupted. Any business that would have been in order at the original meeting may be considered and acted upon in the adjourned meeting. Likewise, any business not in order at the previous meeting may not be brought before the adjourned meeting.

The bylaws of your assembly may also provide for an *annual meeting*. Most assemblies elect officers at their annual meetings, hear annual reports of the officers and committees and conduct any ordinary business that may arise.

The term *executive session* refers to any meeting or part of a meeting that is held in secret. The types of business that are usually conducted in executive session include disciplinary procedures; discussion of the assembly's involvement in legal actions; personnel matters; consideration of bids for goods, services, or property; and other delicate matters whose open discussion would be disadvantageous to the assembly or harmful to its reputation or that of its members. Only members of an assembly and persons invited by the assembly may be present during an executive session. The minutes of an executive session may be read and approved only in executive session.

The Essential Ingredients of a Meeting

In order to conduct a legal meeting of an organization, you must have four things:

1. Previous notice of the meeting.
2. The minimum officers of a chairman and a secretary.
3. A quorum of members.
4. An order of business.

Previous Notice

Every member of an organization has the right to attend and participate in meetings of the organization. Since you cannot attend a meeting you do not know is taking place, the first requirement for holding a legal meeting is *previous notice* to every member that there will be a meeting.

Previous notice for regular meetings is covered by establishing the day, time, and place of meetings in the assembly's bylaws or articles of incorporation. Since you are presumed to have read your own bylaws, any provisions for meetings in your bylaws constitute previous notice for those meetings.

Previous notice for special meetings is issued by the *Call of the Meeting.* Your bylaws should say who may call a special meeting and how and when the call of a special meeting should be given. For example, under your bylaws' article on meetings there could be a section that says:

Section _____. Special meetings shall be called by the Chairman of the Board of Elders upon the written request of ten members of the congregation. The date, time, place, and purpose of the meeting shall be stated in the call. At least two weeks notice of the meeting shall be given by printing the call of the meeting in the church newsletter or by reading it during the Sunday morning worship service.

The call of a special meeting should look something like this:

A special meeting of the congregation will be held on Thursday, May 7, 1986 at 7:00 P.M. in the fellowship hall to consider sponsoring a Birthright Counseling Center.

> Barton W. Stone
> Chairman
> Board of Elders

Previous notice of an adjourned meeting is covered by adoption of a motion to *Fix the Time to Which to Adjourn* at the original meeting.

Minimum Officers

Every parliamentary body must have a chairman to enforce the rules and a secretary to record the proceedings. Your group may add whatever other officers it needs, but an assembly cannot function without these two. Even a mass meeting, which has no permanent officers, must elect a temporary chairman and a secretary (who are called a chairman or secretary *pro tem*) before it can conduct business.

The Chairman. The chairman should be chosen chiefly for his presiding skills. Even if he has an able parliamentarian to advise him, he must himself have a solid grasp of the rules of order and be able to apply them with authority and grace. The presiding officer must also be able to help members in understanding proceedings and in using correct procedure. A president who is short on administrative skills can call on others to help him administrate. But a president who cannot preside is courting disaster when he assumes the chair.

If you are the presiding officer of a deliberative assembly, your principal duties are:

1. Call the meeting to order on time, and determine that a quorum is present.
2. Announce the business before the assembly in its proper order.
3. Recognize members entitled to the floor.
4. State and put to a vote all questions that properly come before the assembly.
5. Answer parliamentary inquiries relating to pending business and assist members in using correct procedure.
6. Make clear, decisive rulings on all questions of order.
7. Declare the meeting adjourned (when so voted, or when the time previously established comes, or in an emergency).
8. Set an example to the assembly in fairness, courtesy, and obedience to the rules.

Those are your duties. Now, what do you need to know and be able to do to carry out those duties?

1. Know the rules. Develop a broad knowledge of parliamentary procedure. Learn the chart of motions in the front of this book. Become familiar with *Robert's Rules of Order Newly Revised* or whatever parliamentary manual your group uses. Know your own bylaws and any special rules adopted by your assembly. If you do not know how to handle a particular item of business, look it up or ask someone who knows, but do find out. You must know the rules. If you have a good parliamentarian, make a habit of conferring with him *before* the meeting. Seek his help in identifying potential trouble spots in the agenda and how you plan to handle them.

Your effectiveness as a chairman depends in large part on how well you know the bylaws, rules, and parliamentary authority of your assembly.

2. *Always know exactly what's going on in the meeting.* Members can afford not to know everything that is going on in a meeting, but not the chair. A good presiding officer always knows exactly what is happening. The biggest part of this job is keeping up with pending motions until they are disposed of. You must keep track of every motion on the floor. You must always know exactly what motions are pending and at what stage in the parliamentary process each motion is. Is that member making a motion or debating a motion that is already pending? Are you supposed to state the question or put the question now? Is that member making a *Parliamentary Inquiry,* which you should answer, or a *Point of Order,* on which you should rule?

If you do not know what a member is doing, ask him. If you ever lose track of the proceedings, quietly ask your parliamentarian or secretary for help. But you must always know what is and what should be happening in the meeting.

3. *Use the correct parliamentary language for every action.* Understanding what is going on in the meeting is not enough. You must make the members understand what is going on. Good chairmen accomplish this by using the correct parliamentary terms for every action, especially when handling motions. Pay attention to what the chairman says in each of the examples in the book. Do not simply copy what you may have heard other chairmen say. Look it up.

"All in favor say 'aye'. All opposed, the like sign." So what does that mean? That opponents of a motion are supposed to say 'aye' too? (Don't laugh, I've seen it happen.) "Do I hear a second?" I don't know, do you? Do not ask us questions about your hearing. "I do not think you can make that motion now." Are you expressing an opinion or making a ruling? There is a difference. "We are going to vote on the motion now." Which motion? These bad habits of language are inelegant and, what is worse, confusing. Learn the correct terms for every action and use them.

Never speak of yourself in the first person. Never say, "I," "me," "my," or "mine." You are *the chair.* While presiding at a meeting, or even when discussing some action you took while presiding, never ever refer to yourself by any other term than "the chair."

Except in the smallest and most informal assemblies, avoid calling a member by name and never address him as "you." Everyone in a parliamentary assembly is addressed and referred to in the third person. Address officers and committee chairmen by their titles—"the registration secretary," "the chairman of the committee," "the executive director." Address speakers as "the speaker," "the gentleman," "the lady," "the brother who just spoke," "the sister who made the motion." The rule is: Avoid names whenever possible. For example:

WRONG: "I think your motion violates the bylaws, so I'm going to rule it out of order."
RIGHT: "The gentleman's motion violates Bylaw Three; therefore, the chair rules that it is out of order."

Does that sound impersonal? That's just the point. This careful, formal way of referring to yourself and to other members keeps personalities out of the proceedings. It also emphasizes your authority as the chair. Even members who may not like you or who disagree with you are bound by the rules to respect the chair. Hence, your consistent use of "the chair" when referring to yourself is a subtle reminder of the legitimate authority you exercise while presiding.

The use of the exact parliamentary language for every action makes that action clear to every member and gives the proceedings an air of formality and courtesy that will discourage challenges to your authority and rough treatment of other officers and members.

4. Assist members in using correct procedure. A good chairman not only adheres to the correct parliamentary rules and customs himself but also helps members by suggesting the correct language or procedure when they need assistance.

For example, suppose that during debate on a main motion a member says: "Mr. Chairman, can we go ahead and vote on this motion right now?" Since the member obviously wants to order the *Previous Question,* the chair should assist him in framing his motion. Such an exchange could proceed:

CHAIR: "Does the member wish to move the previous question?

MEMBER: "I don't know, I just want to go ahead and vote on this motion from the missions committee."

CHAIR: "The member's motion is to order the previous question. Is there a second? . . ."

Or, a member could say:

MEMBER: "Mr. Chairman, I think the finance committee ought to take a look at this."

CHAIR: "Is the member moving to refer the motion to the finance committee?"

MEMBER: "I believe so."

CHAIR: "Is there a second to the motion to refer? . . . (Second) . . . It has been moved and seconded that the pending question be referred to the finance committee."

Or,

MEMBER: "Mr. Chairman, we ought to take out that last sentence in the motion; it's not accurate."

CHAIR: "Is the member moving to amend the motion by striking the last sentence?"

MEMBER: "Yes."

CHAIR: "Is there a second to the amendment? . . . (Second) . . . It has been moved and seconded to amend the motion by striking the last sentence."

5. Make clear, decisive rulings, and be quick about it. When a member raises a *Point of Order,* make a clear, decisive, immediate ruling on the point. Say, "The point of order is well taken," and order whatever action is necessary to correct the problem, or say "The point of order is not well taken," and briefly explain why. If anything else starts to come out of your mouth, bite off the end of your tongue.

Every good chairmen occasionally make mistakes. When a member calls attention to an error through a *Point of Order,* you in no way lose face by ruling his point well taken. To the contrary, your prompt action in correcting the error will enhance your stature among the members. If the member is mistaken in raising the *Point of Order,* your ruling against the point will politely, but firmly, dispatch his challenge. If the member wishes, he may appeal the ruling. But you must first make it.

To be prompt in your rulings does not mean to let yourself be rushed. If you need to consult your parliamentarian or refer to a rule, do so. And do not let the assembly push you. Do not allow any member to raise a second *Point of Order* until you have ruled on the first.

Remember that points of order are incidental to the assembly's business. Time spent in handling them is time not spent in handling the substantive matters for which the members have met. Be quick in giving clear, decisive rulings.

6. Be fair. A presiding officer must show no evidence of favoritism, self-interest, or the indulgence of his own likes and dislikes while in the chair. He must maintain a strict impartiality in conducting the assembly's business. Except in small boards and committees, he is not allowed to participate in debate, and even then, he must take pains to be fair in giving a full hearing to differing views.

This does not mean that you cannot have a viewpoint or that there are no circumstances in which you may make known your views. One of the most partisan acts that can take place in a meeting, making or breaking a tie vote, is the chairman's prerogative. But you must hold both friends and foes to a strict adherence to the rules.

7. Be firm, but gracious. The chair must keep order. The members need to see that someone is in charge of things, that the leader they have chosen to preside over their affairs is going to insist that every member adhere to the rules.

At the same time, they do not want a dictator. Never forget that you exercise the powers of the chair as a servant of the assembly. You must enforce the rules, but do so with courtesy and tact.

8. Be equipped. Take the following items with you to

the meeting and keep them within reach while you preside:

1. A gavel
2. A copy of the bylaws and any other rules of the assembly
3. A copy of the parliamentary authority (usually *Robert's Rules of Order Newly Revised*)
4. The chart on *Rules and Precedence of Motions* printed in the front of this book
5. The agenda
6. A list of all standing and special committees, their members and chairmen
7. If a special meeting, a copy of the call of the meeting
8. Any other papers pertaining to the business scheduled for that session
9. A legal pad for keeping track of motions as they are presented
10. Unless you have a timekeeper, a timer.

When I preside at large or especially important meetings, such as conventions, or work as the parliamentarian for another presiding officer, I write a complete script for the meeting. The script is an expanded version of the agenda that shows each item of business I expect to come before the meeting, along with the *exact words* the chairman is supposed to use in handling that item of business. If there are any rules or bylaws peculiar to that item or class of business, I include a brief note on the rule, including where it is found (down to the page number). I keep this scripted agenda in a divided, loose-leaf notebook. The notebook also contains a copy of the assembly's bylaws, along with my marginal notes on the bylaws, any special rules of the assembly, and any other documents I may need to consult during the meeting.

Is writing a script of a meeting a lot of trouble? Yes, it is, but it pays. With a well-written script, you do not hesitate or grope for the right words. You have the correct parliamentary language right in front of you. There will be enough unexpected turns of events in any large meeting to test your parliamentary skills and your wits. Having a script to guide you through the routine matters frees your mind to think about the unexpected. I even try to anticipate potential trouble spots in the agenda and write out what I will say if and when those problems arise. Other than having a good working knowledge of parliamentary procedure, which you should be working on anyway, writing and using a script will do more to make you an efficient, accurate, and confident presiding officer than any other preparatory step I know.

The Secretary. The other essential officer of a deliberative assembly is the secretary. An assembly may or may not have a secretary to handle administrative matters, but it cannot do without a recording secretary or clerk.

The secretary's most important job is to make and keep a record, called *minutes,* of what is done at every meeting. When approved by the assembly, these minutes become the official, legal record of the assembly's proceedings.

The opening paragraph of the minutes should record:

1. The name of the group holding the meeting
2. The date, hour, and place of the meeting
3. The kind of meeting (regular, special, adjourned, annual)
4. The name of the presiding officer
5. The reading and approval of the minutes of the previous meeting

6. If a special meeting, a copy of the call of the meeting.

The body of the minutes should contain a separate paragraph for each item of business that comes before the meeting. There should be an entry for:

I. Each main motion or restorative motion, including:
   A. The exact wording of the motion or resolution
   B. The name of the maker of the motion
   C. How the motion was disposed of
   D. If the motion was temporarily disposed of (referred to committee, postponed, laid on the table, etc.), any amendments and adhering secondary motions that were pending
   E. If a counted vote was taken, the number voting on each side.
II. Each committee report, including:
   A. The name of the reporting committee
   B. The name of the committee member who presented the report
   C. A brief summary of the report
   D. What action the assembly took on it
III. All notices of future action
IV. All points of order and appeals, together with the chair's reasons for his ruling.

The last paragraph should state the hour the meeting adjourned. The secretary should sign the minutes. When they are later approved by the assembly, the secretary should write the date of their approval and his initials at the bottom of the page. The procedure for approving minutes is in the section on *Reading and Approval of Minutes* later in this chapter.

Secretaries err in recording too much, recording too little, or recording the wrong things. Remember that minutes are supposed to be a record of what the assembly *did*, not what the members *said*. The most common errors in recording minutes are:

1. Failing to record the name of the organization that held the meeting
2. Failing to record the year as well as the day and month of the meeting
3. Failing to record who called the meeting to order and presided
4. Failing to record *Points of Order* and *Appeals*, along with the chairman's reasons for each ruling
5. Failing to record motions adopted by unanimous consent
6. Failing to record counted votes
7. Failing to record previous notices given at the meeting
8. Failing to record the fact and the time of adjournment
9. Including the name of the seconder of motions
10. Including detailed accounts of subsidiary motions that did not make a difference in the final disposition of a main motion
11. Including remarks made in debate
12. Including an excessive description of the program or other non-business aspects of the meeting.

The secretary should also keep a copy of all reports given by officers and committees, the official membership roll, and whatever other records the bylaws or the assembly may require.

Prior to each meeting, the secretary should assist the chairman in preparing the agenda by informing him of all business postponed to or scheduled for that meeting and any unfinished business that should be considered.

Quorum of Members

A *quorum* is the minimum number or percentage of members who must be present in order to conduct a meeting. The rule is: no quorum, no meeting. The purpose of having a quorum is to prevent an unrepresentatively small group of members from taking action that binds the entire organization.

Your bylaws should say what number or percentage of members constitutes a quorum for your assembly. For most groups, with changing membership rolls, a number is more convenient than a percentage, which is confusing because it requires a re-computation of the quorum for every change in membership. A good place to set the quorum is just below the number of members who usually attend your meetings. If you set it much lower, you run the risk of putting the assembly's decision-making powers into the hands of an unrepresentative minority. If the quorum is much larger, you may be unable to hold a meeting because you cannot get a quorum.

Usually, your bylaws do not specify a quorum, it is automatically set at a majority for the entire membership.

The chairman is responsible for determining that a quorum is present before he calls a meeting to order. A quorum is presumed to be present unless the chair or a member notices it is not and says something about it. If the chair notices the absence of a quorum, it is his duty to declare the fact. Any member who notices the absence of a quorum may raise a *Point of Order* to that effect. For example:

MEMBER: "Mr. Chairman, I rise to a point of order."
CHAIR: "State your point of order."
MEMBER: "Mr. Chairman, I suggest the absence of a quorum."
CHAIR: "The members will rise and remain standing until counted."

The chair must then count the members on the floor to establish whether a quorum is present. He may appoint tellers to assist him in taking the count.

If a quorum is present, the chair rules the *Point of Order* not well-taken and proceeds with business. In the absence of a quorum, an assembly can do only three things: (1) adjourn; (2) make provisions for an adjourned meeting by adopting a motion to *Fix the Time To Which to Adjourn;* or (3) recess and go hunt up enough members to make a quorum. There is a fourth, rather chancy alternative. If there is some urgent business that must be acted upon immediately, the members present may take emergency action and hope that a later meeting, with a quorum, will ratify their action. That later meeting has no obligation to ratify the emergency action, and the members of the quorumless meeting assume all risk for whatever they do.

Order of Business

The last essential ingredient of a meeting is an *order of business*. The order of business for a particular meeting is called the *agenda*. An agenda usually specifies only the order in which classes of business will be taken up, but it may assign times to each item of business. An assembly may specify an order of business in its bylaws. If it does not, the standard order of business is:

1. Call to order; opening ceremonies
2. Reading and approval of minutes

3. Reports of officers, boards, and standing committees
4. Reports of special committees
5. Special orders
6. Unfinished business and general orders
7. New business
8. Adjournment.

Call to Order. When the scheduled time for the meeting arrives, the chairman steps to the podium, raps the gavel lightly, and says:

> CHAIR: "The meeting will come to order."

The call to order is usually followed by an invocation and any other customary opening ceremonies, such as pledging allegiance to the flag.

Reading and Approval of Minutes. Until the assembly approves a set of minutes, they are simply the secretary's notes as to what took place at a meeting. Once approved, they become the official record of the assembly's proceedings.

At each regular meeting, the secretary reads the minutes of the previous regular meeting and any special or adjourned meetings held in the mean time. Occasionally, someone may move to "dispense with the reading of the minutes." If adopted, this motion simply postpones the reading and approval of the minutes to a later time. It does not dispense with the necessity of approving those minutes.

The procedure for reading and approving minutes:

> CHAIR: "The secretary will read the minutes. . . .
> *(The secretary reads the minutes.)* . . . Are
> there any corrections to the minutes? . . .
> *(Pause)* . . . If there are no corrections *(no*

further corrections), the minutes are approved as read (as corrected)."

Corrections to and approval of the minutes are usually handled by general consent. If your secretary distributes printed copies of the minutes to the members, you may omit reading the minutes aloud and approve them as follows:

CHAIR: "You have a printed copy of the minutes. Are there any corrections? . . . If not, then the minutes are approved as printed."

The secretary should write the date the minutes are approved at the bottom of the page and initial it.

Most members pay little attention to the approval of minutes, at least until they need some crucial bit of information about a previous action of the assembly and are foiled by an inaccurate or incomplete set of minutes. Pay particular attention to how the minutes state action on questions in which you have an interest.

Reports of Officers, Boards, and Standing Committees. The chairman should know ahead of time which officers and committees have reports to make. He calls on those with reports by saying:

CHAIR: "May we have the treasurer's report?"
                           Or,
          "The chair recognizes Mrs. Laura Moody, chairman of the Ladies Auxiliary, for a report."

The treasurer's report follows the reading and approval of the minutes, then those of any other officers who have reports. Boards and standing committees report in the order in which they are listed in the bylaws.

Any recommendations from an officer, board, or committee should be made in the form of a motion. If an officer makes a recommendation, it is customary for another member to make a motion to carry out the recommendation as soon as the officer has finished his report. When a committee makes a recommendation, the chairman of the committee should immediately move its adoption. The assembly then considers that question before proceeding with the rest of the committee's report or any further recommendations. For example:

COMMITTEE "Mr. Chairman, the building commit-
CHAIRMAN: tee recommends 'That the church approve the contract with Randy Howard and Company to pave the church parking lot at a cost of $9,500.' On behalf of the committee, I move the adoption of this recommendation."

CHAIR: "The question is on the adoption of the Finance Committee's recommendation. Is there any discussion?"

Committee recommendations are treated as main motions. They are debatable, amendable, and may have any applicable subsidiary motions applied to them.

Reports of Special Committees. Special committees who are prepared or were instructed to report at this meeting are called on in the order in which they were appointed. Their reports are handled the same way as those of standing committees.

Special Orders. You may remember from the section on the motion to *Postpone to a Certain Time* that there are three kinds of special orders:

1. Special orders that have no particular time set for their consideration
2. Special orders that do have a particular time set for their consideration
3. *The Special Order* for a meeting.

A special order set for a particular time is taken up at that time. The Special Order for a meeting is taken up as soon as the minutes have been approved. These two classes of special orders are treated in the section on *Exceptions to the Regular Order of Business* in this chapter.

The place in the standard order of business designated for *Special Orders* is for the first type of special orders: those not set for particular times. Since a special order is usually a motion made at a previous meeting that has been postponed to the current meeting, no one needs to make the motion again. When the time for considering the special order arrives, the chair states the motion to the assembly for consideration. For example:

CHAIR: "At the last meeting, the motion to invite Dr. Walter Scott to hold an evangelistic meeting was made a special order for this meeting. The motion reads as follows: 'That the church invite Dr. Walter Scott to hold an evangelistic meeting October 5-11, 1986, and that a free-will offering for Dr. Scott be received each night of the meeting.' The question is on the adoption of the motion. Is there any discussion?"

Unfinished Business and General Orders. *Unfinished business* is any item of business left over from a previous meeting that adjourned before completing its agenda. Only assemblies that meet at least quarterly can carry over unfinished business to the next regular meeting. The term *unfinished business* is more accurate than *old business*, which suggests the dredging up of matters the assembly has already decided.

After unfinished business comes general orders, which are usually motions postponed to the present meeting without specifying a time for their consideration.

The chair would handle business in this category like this:

> CHAIR: "Under Unfinished Business and General Orders, the first item of business is the motion relating to _____."

The chairman should never ask, "Is there any unfinished business?" He should know. If there are any items of unfinished business or general orders to be taken up, then the minutes of the previous meeting will show it. If they do not, there is none, and the chairman simply skips this category of business.

New Business. When all orders of the day and items of unfinished business are finished, the chair asks:

> CHAIR: "Is there any new business?"

You may then introduce any new items of business by following the basic procedure for handling motions explained in Chapter 2.

New business is in order until it is all done, the assembly votes to adjourn, or a previously scheduled time for adjournment arrives. An impatient chairman has no right to rush through the proceedings. As long as you have legitimate business to bring before the assembly and are prompt in claiming the floor, no one can deprive you of the right to make your motion. If the majority is anxious to go home, they can always vote to do so.

Adjournment. The chair declares the meeting adjourned when: (1) The assembly adopts a motion to *Adjourn;* (2) A pre-scheduled time for adjournment arrives and no motion to extend the time is adopted; or (3) There appears to be no further business.

When a member moves to *Adjourn,* after another member seconds the motion, the chair says:

> CHAIR: "It has been moved and seconded to adjourn. As many as are in favor of adjourning, say 'aye'. . . . Those opposed, say 'no'. . . . The ayes have it and the motion is carried. The meeting is adjourned."

A pre-scheduled time for adjournment is a special order and is handled like all other special orders set for particular times (see the section on special orders that follows). When the hour of adjournment arrives, the chair says:

> CHAIR: "The hour for adjournment has arrived and time for consideration of the pending question has expired. The question is on _____. *(The chair puts all pending questions to a vote, then declares:)* The meeting is adjourned."

When an assembly has completed its agenda and there appears to be no further business, the chair may adjourn the meeting as follows:

> CHAIR: "Is there any further business? . . . *(Pause)* . . . Since there is no further business, the meeting is adjourned."

Special Orders and Other Exceptions to the Regular Order of Business. An assembly may take up any item of business out of its proper order by adopting a motion to

Suspend the Rules, which is not debatable and requires a two-thirds vote.

For example, suppose a meeting has several lengthy committee reports on the agenda. You have an important item of *new business* to introduce. You do not want to delay consideration of your motion until hours later when members are tired, unattentive, and anxious to go home. If you think your business is important enough that two-thirds of the members would agree to consider your motion before all of the committee reports are done, you could claim the floor between reports and do this:

MEMBER: "Mr. Chairman, I move to suspend the rules and proceed to take up an important item of new business concerning the church's participation in the campaign to strengthen our state's anti-pornography law. *(Second.)*"

CHAIR: "It has been moved and seconded to suspend the rules and proceed to take up the member's motion. *(The chair then puts the question on suspending the rules.)*"

The chair himself may have reason for wanting to take up an item of business before its scheduled time, in which case he may say:

CHAIR: "If there is no objection, the chair proposes at this time to proceed to take up _____. . . . *(Pause)* . . . Without objection, it is so ordered."

In most cases an agenda only specifies the order in which classes of business will be taken up in a meeting. Such an agenda allows members to spend whatever time they deem necessary to handle each item of business. But when as assembly has much business to do and a limited time in which to do it, such as in a convention, the agenda may specify times for the consideration of classes or even individual items of business. Any class or individual item of business scheduled for a specific time becomes a special order, which, with only a few exceptions, interrupts whatever business pending when the time for its consideration arrives.

If an item of business has been made a special order, either by a motion to *Postpone* or by an agenda that assigns specific times to items of business, when the time for considering that special order arrives, the chair announces the fact and puts to a vote any pending questions, without further debate, unless:

A. A member moves to *Extend* the time for consideration of that item, which motion is undebatable and requires a two-thirds vote (but can be done by general consent), or

B. A member moves to *Refer, Postpone,* or *Lay on the Table* the pending business, which motions are amendable, but undebatable, and require a majority vote. (Though *Refer* and *Postpone* are normally debatable motions, they are undebatable here because time for debate has expired.)

The following example illustrates the procedure for clearing the floor to take up a special order set for a particular time. Suppose a report from the Pulpit Committee has been made a special order for 8:00. At 8:00, the chair interrupts debate on the pending question and says:

CHAIR: "Time for consideration of the question has expired. The question is on _____. *(The chair then puts the question on the pending motion.)* The chair recognizes R. John Smith, Chairman of the Pulpit Committee, for a report."

If, when the chair announces that time for consideration of the pending question has expired, members move and second an extension of time, the chair says:

CHAIR: "It has been moved and seconded to extend the time for consideration of the question." *(The chair then puts the question on extending time.)*

Or, the chair himself may suggest an extension of time:

CHAIR: "If there is no objection, the time for consideration of the question will be extended five minutes. . . . *(Pause)* . . . Without objection it is so ordered."

If the time for considering the pending question is extended, then the special order waits until the extension has expired. When time is up again, the chair announces that fact and proceeds to put the pending question to a vote and move on to the special order.

If an item of business has been designated as The Special Order for a meeting, it is always taken up immediately after the reading and approval of minutes.

6
Committees

Nothing is impossible, until it is sent to a committee.

God so loved the world, that he didn't send a committee.

In spite of all the jokes about committees, they are among the most useful devices of parliamentary procedure. Good committees can help an assembly manage its affairs more efficiently, make better decisions, and put the special talents and interests of individual members to their fullest use. Much of the business of large assemblies consists of approving what their committees have done.

Writing at the turn of the century, then Speaker of the House of Representatives Thomas B. Reed described the importance of committees:

> The committee is the eye, and ear, and hand, and very often the brain, of the assembly. Freed from the very great inconvenience of numbers, it can study a question, obtain full information, and put the proposed action into proper shape for final decision.[1]

The sixth chapter of Acts describes how the apostles solved the problem of administering the church's benevolent ministry to its widows by calling a congregational meeting and appointing a committee. The church chose seven qualified committeemen to handle the business, the apostles returned to their ministry of preaching and praying, "and the word of God increased; and the number of disciples multiplied in Jerusalem greatly" (Acts 6:7). Note that the creation of a committee to handle a specific task contributed to the overall success of the church's ministry.

What Committees Do

A *committee* is any group of members to whom an assembly has committed some specialized task. Motions or other business matters may be referred to a committee when the assembly needs a small group of selected members to study a matter before acting on it. Committees can also handle delicate matters, such as disciplinary procedures, more discreetly than could a meeting of the entire membership. Committee meetings can also provide a forum for advocates of conflicting views to work out their differences without taking up excessive time in meetings of the assembly.

The three general purposes for which assemblies create committees are:

1. *To study or investigate a matter.* An assembly may instruct a committee to investigate, conduct research, or hold hearings on a question. When so instructed, the committee merely reports its findings, leaving the introduction of any motions to the members of the assembly.

2. *To recommend action.* A committee may be charged with investigating and recommending action on a question. The committee can recommend that a motion be adopted, rejected, amended, postponed to a certain time, or post-

poned indefinitely. It may evaluate amendments that are referred with the motion, or suggest its own.

3. *To take action.* Committees ordinarily possess only the power to recommend action, leaving the assembly itself to adopt any motions that are needed to carry it out. But an assembly may, through its bylaws or a motion, empower a committee to act on its behalf. Most organizations establish standing committees that have jurisdiction over certain classes of business, such as finances, missions, or worship. When a committee has taken some action it was empowered to take, the chairman reports that fact. No further action by the assembly is necessary.

Whatever purposes they serve, committees are instruments of the parent body that creates them. They are subject to the orders of the assembly of which they are a part and may perform only those specific functions authorized by the assembly's bylaws, rules, or motions.

Standing Committees

The chief distinction between the two types of committees is that standing committees are permanent; special committees are temporary.

Standing committees are established to perform some continuing function, such as a finance committee or a nominating committee. Standing committees are usually created by the assembly's bylaws. Your bylaws should have an article that defines each standing committee by specifying:

1. The name of the committee
2. The number of members

3. The number constituting a quorum for committee meetings, if more or less than the automatic quorum of a majority
4. How members are elected or appointed and any special qualifications for membership
5. How the chairman is elected or appointed
6. Terms of office
7. Provisions for filling vacancies
8. The duties and powers of the committee
9. The time and frequency of regular meetings, unless the committee is to arrange its own meetings or meet at the call of the chairman
10. When the committee reports to the assembly.

For example, under the article on committees, your by-laws could have a section that says:

Section _____. A Stewardship Committee composed of the church Treasurer, who shall serve as chairman of the committee, and four deacons shall prepare a budget for the fiscal year beginning the first day of October. With the exception of the Treasurer, who is elected by the congregation, members of the committee shall be elected by the Board of Deacons immediately following each annual meeting of the congregation, and shall serve for a term of one year or until their successors are elected. Vacancies on the committee shall be filled by the Board of Deacons. The committee shall present the budget to the congregation at the regular business meeting in September. The committee may from time to time submit supplements to the budget for the current fiscal year. The committee shall also plan and supervise the church's annual stewardship campaign.

Organizations often make certain officers *ex officio* members of committees. The president is commonly made an ex officio member of all committees except the nominating committee. The term *ex officio* means "by virtue of office or position." Ex officio members have the right, but not the obligation, to attend committee meetings, participate in debate, and vote just as any other member of the committee. They are not counted in the quorum, though.

Special Committees

Special committees cease to exist whenever the task for which they were created is done. They can be created by a motion to *Refer to Committee* or by a main motion to form a committee for some special task. Any motion to create a special committee should state the committee's membership and duties. If the motion does not designate the chairman of the committee, then the first committee member named in the motion creating the committee, or the first member appointed or elected to the committee, is the chairman.

Members of a special committee may be chosen by any of four methods:

1. The maker of the motion creating the committee names its members in his motion.
2. The chair appoints the committee.
3. The chair nominates members who are confirmed by a vote of the assembly.
4. The assembly nominates and elects the committee.

The following example illustrates how a special committee can be created by a motion to *Refer:*

MEMBER: "Mr. Chairman, I move that the motion to purchase new hymnals be referred to a committee of three to be appointed by the chair, with instructions to report at the next regular meeting."

A motion to create a committee that is made while no other motion is pending is a main motion.

Boards

Like standing committees, boards are created by an assembly's bylaws to perform some continuing function. The two special characteristics of boards are: (1) They are usually composed of the officers of an organization and, sometimes, other members elected by the assembly; (2) they are empowered to supervise and carry on the work of the assembly between meetings of the general membership.

If your church or organization has a governing board of elders, deacons, directors, or trustees, your bylaws should contain an article that clearly and exactly defines the composition, powers, and procedures of the board. The bylaws article on the board should contain the ten items of information we recommended for standing committees, *and,* this is important, a section that delineates the powers of the board. If your board only has general supervision of your assembly's business between meetings, that section could say:

Section _____. The Board of (Elders, Deacons, Directors, Trustees, etc.) shall have general supervision of the affairs of the (Assembly, Church, Convention, Corporation, etc.) between its business meetings, make recommendations to the Assembly, and perform such other duties as these bylaws and the rules of the Assembly specify. The Board shall be subject to the orders of the Assembly, and none of its acts shall conflict with action taken by the Assembly.

Or, if your assembly wishes to turn over all of its business to an elected governing board, that section should say:

Section _____. The Board of (Elders, Directors, etc.) shall have full power and authority over the affairs of the Assembly, except . . . (here the assembly may specify certain classes of business it wishes to reserve to itself).

Do not worry if your bylaws article on the board looks like a set of mini-bylaws. The duties and powers of governing boards need to be very carefully defined.

How Committees Work

Committee meetings are characterized by informality. Most of the committee's work can be conducted without a strict adherence to the parliamentary rules that must govern larger groups. Motions do not require seconds in committee meetings. Committees may informally discuss a subject while no motion is pending. There is no limit on the number of times a committee member may speak, and the chairman himself may make and discuss motions, as long as he does not infringe upon the right of other members to speak.

Committees often decide matters by general consent. If, after a period of informal discussion, an action appears to be clear to everyone, the chairman may put a question to a vote without the formal introduction of a motion. The motion to reconsider is always in order in committee meetings and can be moved by any member of the committee, whether he voted with the prevailing side or not.

Writing Reports

Committee reports should be written and filed with the secretary of the assembly at the time the committee gives its oral report. Reports should be worded in the third person. Never say "we find that . . . ," but "the Finance Committee finds that . . . ." The standard form for a committee report with recommendations is:

1. An identification of the committee submitting the report. A standing committee report would begin: "The Missions Committee reports that . . . ." A special committee report would say: "The committee to which was referred the motion on _____ reports that . . . ."

2. A description of how the committee undertook its handling of the matter on which it is reporting. Has the committee prepared this report on its own initiative, or did the assembly refer this matter to the committee? Give specific details, such as the date of referral, the exact wording of any motions and pending amendments that were referred, and any specific instructions given to the committee. The committee may attach to its report any documents it believes are of significance.

3. The facts uncovered by the committee's research and study and a list of their sources and consultants.

4. The committee's findings or conclusions on the matter, along with arguments in favor of whatever recommendations it is making.

5. A clear statement of the committee's recommendations for action by the assembly. Recommendations should always be reported out in the form of a motion. The committee chairman should move the

adoption of each recommendation at the conclusion of the report.

Usually the chairman signs and makes the oral presentation of the report on behalf of the committee. If the report deals with important or controversial matters, all the members who concur with the report should sign it. Committee members who disagree with a report may submit a *minority report*. When given, the minority report follows the report of the committee. The assembly may refuse permission to present a minority report. If allowed, a minority report is treated as a substitute amendment to the committee report. The member presenting the report should begin this way:

MEMBER: "Mr. Chairman, the undersigned minority of the Missions Committee, not agreeing with the majority, wishes to express their views on. . . ."

The report is signed by the dissenting members and their names are read at the conclusion of the oral report. Though a report by members not agreeing with the majority is called a "minority report," the report of the majority is not called "the majority report." The proper term is "the committee report."

Presenting Reports

A committee may present its report by having the chairman read it to the assembly or by distributing printed copies of the report to the members with the chairman calling attention to significant portions of the report before moving any recommendations.

The following are two examples of how committee reports are presented:

A Report from a Standing Committee.

MEMBER: "Mr. Chairman, the Building Committee submits the following report on the acquisition of land for our new church building:

"Six months ago, the church purchased five acres of land on which to build a new building and to relocate the church. Since then our consultants, Goodman Church Builders, have completed a feasibility study for the project. The committee has twice met with Goodman Church Builders and has held two committee meetings to discuss their findings.

"The committee is delighted to report that the feasibility study's projection of the congregation's growth over the next ten years is one-third greater than the committee's original estimate and that the initial purchase of five acres of land will be insufficient for the church's long-term growth. The committee has also located a ten-acre tract of land within one-half mile of the present site that the owner has agreed to sell to the church at ten percent below fair market value as determined by an independent appraiser.

"The committee therefore recommends the adoption of the following motion: 'That the Building Committee be authorized to list for sale with Cooper Realty the five-acre tract of land originally purchased for relocation of the church and to negotiate the purchase of the ten-acre tract now owned by Isacc Errett, with instructions to report to the congregation before final contracts are signed.'

"Mr. Chairman, on behalf of the committee, I move the adoption of the motion just read."

A Report from a Special Committee.

MEMBER: "Mr. Chairman, the committee to which was referred the motion to purchase new hymnals submits the following report:

"The committee has met three times since the last congregational meeting. The committee found that 210 of the hymnals currently in use are in good to excellent condition and that 90 are badly worn and should be replaced. the committee believes that the congregation also needs an additional 75 hymnals to meet current needs and our projected growth over the next two to three years.

"The committee also reviewed new hymnals from five publishers and found the Broadman Hymnal currently in use still the best hymnal for our congregation.

"The committee therefore recommends 'That the congregation purchase 165 Broadman Hymnals.'

"Mr. Chairman, on behalf of the committee, I move the adoption of the motion, just read."

Remember that recommendations, when made, are the heart of a report. Whatever action the committee recommends must be made as a clearly stated motion, which the committee chairman moves for adoption by the assembly at the conclusion of his report.

Acting on Reports

What an assembly does with a report depends upon the purpose of the report. If a report is for information only, nothing needs to be done except receive the report. If the committee has recommendations for action, the assembly debates and votes on those recommendations. If the committee is reporting on a motion referred to it in a previous meeting, the committee's report in effect returns the motion to the assembly for further consideration and action. The committee may report the motion with or without amendments, with or without a recommendation to adopt or reject the motion, and the assembly takes it from there.

An assembly *receives* a report when it allows the report to be formally presented in oral or written form by the committee chairman. In parliamentary procedure, receiving a report simply means to allow it to be presented. Receiving a report does not adopt, approve, endorse, or imply agreement with anything said in the report. Some assemblies have the bad habit of moving to receive reports after they have just heard them. Such motions are superfluous, since the assembly received the reports when they allowed the committees to give them.

Once a report has been received, it belongs to the assembly. The reporting committee may not amend it further, unless the assembly again refers the matter to the committee.

If a report contains information only with no specific recommendations for action, then no further action is necessary.

If the assembly is not satisfied with the report, if it is

confusing or incomplete, it may be referred back to the
same committee, or to another committee, for additional
work.

When a committee report contains recommendations,
they are moved by the committee chairman at the end of
the report, following the procedure discussed in the section on committee reports in Chapter 5. The assembly
may adopt, reject, amend, or otherwise dispose of any recommendations proposed by the committee.

A motion to *Adopt* a report, in contrast to adopting a single recommendation, should be made only when the
maker of the motion wishes to make every assertion contained in the report the official statement of the assembly
as a whole. The motion to *Adopt* an entire report is a main
motion. It may be made by the committee chairman or by
another member at the conclusion of the report.

Discharging a Committee

When an assembly refers a motion to a committee, the
assembly itself cannot consider that question again, or
any other motion involving essentially the same question,
until the committee submits its report on that motion. The
assembly can, however, take the matter out of the committee's hands by adopting a motion to *Discharge a Committee*. Though this motion is not listed on the chart of
motions in the front of the book, the rules governing it are
identical to the motion to *Amend or Rescind Something
Previously Adopted*.

The assembly may discharge a committee anytime
after referring a matter to it and before the committee has
made its final report. Since the motion reverses a previous
action, it ordinarily requires a two-thirds vote, a majority
vote with previous notice, or a majority vote of the entire
membership. If the committee fails to report when it was

instructed to do so or if the assembly is considering a partial report of the committee, then a motion to *Discharge* the committee can be adopted by a simple majority vote, without previous notice.

The motion is made this way for a standing committee:

MEMBER: "Mr. Chairman, I move that the Building Committee be discharged from further consideration of the motion to renovate the baptistry."

For a special committee, the member says:

MEMBER: "Mr. Chairman, I move that the committee to which was referred the motion to renovate the baptistry be discharged."

The chair announces the result of an affirmative vote on a motion to discharge this way:

CHAIR: "There are two-thirds in the affirmative and the committee is discharged. The question is now on the motion 'That the church renovate the baptistry.'"

When a standing committee is discharged, the committee continues in existence. It is simply discharged from handling the particular matter the assembly took from it. When a special committee is discharged from handling the matter for which it was created, it ceases to exist.

Convention Committees

Most *conventions* are an assembly of *delegates* who represent constituent units of an organization and act in the name of the entire group. Some conventions consist of *messengers* who represent only themselves. If your church has regional, state, or national conventions, the bylaws at each level (regional bylaws for regional conventions, national bylaws for national conventions) should define the powers and duties of the convention, qualifications for delegates or messengers, how they are chosen, and whatever other provisions are necessary for the operation of the convention.

Each convention, even the annual conventions of a permanent organization, is a separate voting body. The only way one convention can bind another is through a permanent bylaw that continues in effect from year to year. Because each gathering of delegates is a separate body, a convention must organize itself as a deliberative assembly before it can conduct any business. It does this at the first meeting of the first day of the convention by adopting the reports of three committees: the *Credentials Committee,* the *Rules Committee,* and the *Program Committee.* The reports are usually adopted in that order. Once the delegates have adopted reports form these three committees, they are officially organized as a convention and may transact business. All three reports are debatable and amendable. The Rules Committee's report requires a two-thirds vote. The other two reports require only a majority vote.

The *Credentials Committee,* sometimes called the *Registration Committee,* registers delegates or messengers, verifies their credentials, and presents to the convention a list of registered delegates. Once adopted, this credentials report becomes the official roll of voting members of the convention.

The *Rules Committee* drafts and presents to the convention a set of standing rules. When adopted, these standing rules apply to the conduct of business for that convention only. Some national conventions provide permanent rules for their assemblies in their bylaws. If this is the case with your convention, the report of the Rules Committee may be omitted because a permanent set of rules is already in place.

The *Program Committee* plans and proposes a complete order of business for the convention. Once adopted, this order of business constitutes the convention's agenda.

Your convention may have different names for these three essential committees. Your convention may also have other committees to serve the particular needs of your assembly. These committees should be denied and described in your bylaws and convention standing rules.

Note

1. Thomas B. Reed, *Reed's Rules* (Chicago: Rand, McNally and Co., 1899), p. 53.

7
Bylaws

I once served as the interim preacher of a small rural church not far from the college where I taught. For twenty years the church's leadership has consisted of a series of part-time preachers and two lay elders, Sam and Fred. Early on in my ministry there, I asked Sam for a copy of the church's bylaws. He said there were none.

I asked when and how the church elected its officers. Sam said that when he and Fred became elders, they assumed the office carried a life term. Since Fred was also the church treasurer and Bible school superintendent, and Fred's wife was the church secretary, and Sam pretty much took charge of everything else except the preaching, all of the available church offices had been filled for quite some time, and no vacancies were expected in the near future.

I asked who approved the church budget. They didn't have a budget. Fred just deposited whatever showed up in the collection plate in the bank and wrote checks for all the regular expenses, such as utility bills and the preacher's salary. When anything came up that involved spending money, Sam and Fred got together and took care of it. Occasionally, they would take major decisions, such as calling a new preacher, to the congregation.

In a way, the system worked. The bills were paid, the

church lawn was mowed, the building was cleaned, and every Sunday and Wednesday the congregation showed up for services. But in another, more important sense, the system didn't work. The church was stagnant. Few newcomers were ever added to the fellowship. As children of members grew into adults, instead of being challenged to roles of leadership and service in the congregation, most of them just slipped away from the church altogether.

I'm not about to suggest that a set of bylaws was the cure-all for this church's problems. But the process of drafting bylaws did two things for these folks. First, it made the church stop and look at exactly how their business was done, think about how it ought to be done, and make some deliberate choices. Second, it provided the congregation itself the opportunity to give their conscious, written consent to how their affairs were to be conducted. It took almost a year to get this seventy-five year old church to adopt its first set of bylaws.

They kept Fred and Sam as elders, but elected some new leaders to work with them. Other members went to work on several useful new committees. At their first annual congregational meeting the church adopted goals for the year and a budget. In short, members got involved. The church no longer conducted its business by inertia and default. They knew who was doing what and why. In three years the church tripled in membership, giving increased four-fold, and the church commenced a building program to accommodate their new growth.

As we noted in the first chapter, your church business meetings will be governed by some set of rules. They might not be written down. They might be made up as you go along. They might be illegal, unscriptural, inefficient, or unfair. But your meetings will be conducted by somebody's stated or unstated rules of procedure.

In order to exist as a permanent organization and conduct business in a fair, efficient, and legal fashion, an assembly must have a basic set of written rules that defines the rights and duties of members, the structure of the assembly, and the basic guidelines for the management of its affairs. These basic rules are called *bylaws*. In unincorporated assemblies, they are the highest legal body of rules governing the assembly and guiding its business.[1] In incorporated assemblies their authority falls just below that of the corporate charter.

Some assemblies divide their basic rules into a "Constitution" and "Bylaws." Under such an arrangement, the constitution contains those rules the assembly regards as most important and is usually made more difficult to amend than the bylaws. Other assemblies put their basic rules in a single document called the "Constitution and Bylaws." The preferred practice now is to have a single document simply called the "Bylaws."

Good bylaws are an effective tool to guide members in exercising their basic rights and duties and to help an assembly conduct its affairs in a fair, efficient, and orderly manner. In this chapter we will look at how to draft a good set of bylaws and how to keep it in working order through amendments and periodic revisions.

Steps in Drafting or Revising Bylaws

Step One: The Assembly Establishes a Committee on Bylaws.

Since drafting or revising bylaws is often a complex job, the initial draft should be prepared by a committee. Some assemblies have a standing committee on bylaws to periodically examine the bylaws for revision and to review amendments to the bylaws proposed by members. As with other standing committees, a committee on bylaws may be established by providing for it in the article of your bylaws that defines standing committees. If your assembly does not have a standing committee on bylaws, a special committee may be appointed by any of the methods for appointing special committees described in chapter six.

The committee on bylaws should include the most prudent and knowledgeable members of the assembly. It is also wise to include opinion leaders and other members with special interests in the assembly's rules. It is better that those members have the opportunity to express their points of view in the committee rather than to consume much time debating the bylaws when they come before the assembly. Don't be concerned if the committee ends up being rather large. The more representative the committee is of the assembly's leadership as a whole, the more likely that the proposed bylaws will reflect the assembly's needs and be adopted without extensive debate and amendment when proposed.

If your organization is large or its structure complex, the services of a professional parliamentarian to advise the committee will prove helpful.[2] If your church or organization is incorporated, any proposed bylaws should be reviewed by an attorney. Since an incorporated society's charter or articles of incorporation supercede its bylaws, the bylaws must not conflict with the charter.

Step Two: The Committee Discovers What the Assembly Needs.

The Greek statesman, Solon, was responsible for sweeping changes in the constitution and laws of ancient Athens. When his reforms were criticized, Solon himself acknowledged that his legal code fell short of perfection.

When asked if he had given the Athenians the best possible laws, he replied, "No, but I have given them the best they could receive."

A bylaws committee must carefully consider the needs of the people who will actually receive and use the bylaws they draft. The committee's job is not to draft the perfect, universal set of bylaws, but to draft the best working document for the particular assembly whose business that document will govern.

Yogi Berra once remarked that "you can observe a lot just by watching." The work of a bylaws committee should be based on careful observation of the assembly for which it is drafting bylaws. The last thing any church or organization needs is an abstract set of rules that fails to address the real needs of the organization. Too many assemblies have bylaws that have been tucked away in a drawer for twenty years because the document was too cumbersome or inadequate to be of any practical use. If anything, bylaws should be practical.

If the committee has been chosen well, the church leaders who serve on it should have a good idea of the current strengths and weaknesses of the assembly's structure and methods of operation. The committee should also consult widely within the assembly to insure that they produce a helpful, working set of bylaws rather than a cumbersome or irrelevant hindrance. For example, if the treasurer is not on the committee, it would be wise to consult him when drafting the article dealing with his duties and with financial matters. The same would apply to ministers, officers, and other members responsible for various parts of the assembly's operation. Ask how things are done now. Find out what works and what doesn't. Then draft the bylaws so that they preserve what works and fixes what doesn't.

Step Three: The Committee Examines the Existing Documents.

If the assembly already has bylaws, the committee should examine them carefully to determine which parts are adequate and which parts should be changed. If a bylaws article is inadequate for the assembly's needs, why is it inadequate? Why doesn't it say what it needs to say? If an article is thought to be too restrictive, why is it so? What does the assembly need to do that the bylaws prevent it from doing? The committee should review all parts of the bylaws about which the assembly, its officers, or committees have had questions of interpretation.

If you are part of a new assembly that is drafting its first set of bylaws, examine the bylaws of other organizations similar to yours. Shop around. You will probably find good ideas from a number of sources. Be careful, though, to think through ideas you find in other documents. Be sure the provisions you adopt from other assemblies really fit the needs of your own.

In practice, steps two and three will most likely overlap. During the process, though, the committee should carefully and critically examine the existing documents that govern the organization. ·

Step Four: The Drafting Sub-Committee Writes the Initial Draft.

The actual writing of the bylaws should be done by a smaller subcommittee of members selected for their writing skills. The assembly's parliamentarian should work closely with this subcommittee. If the bylaws are expected to be long or if there are several complex articles, separate sub-committees may be appointed to handle various articles.

The drafting sub-committee should pay careful attention to good grammar, clear style, and accurate punctuation. The tips on drafting bylaws later in this chapter and a good parliamentary authority, such as *Robert's Rules of Order Newly Revised*, should prove helpful in writing the draft.

Step Five: The Committee Reviews and Revises the Draft.

When the drafting subcommittee has completed its work, the proposed draft of the bylaws should be reviewed by the full committee. A good set of bylaws usually undergoes several revisions before the subcommittee presents it to the full committee. Even then, the proposed draft will probably require more revision before it is ready to present to the assembly.

H. L. Mencken said: "For every problem, there is a solution which is simple, neat, and wrong." The review stage is the committee's opportunity to check their draft of the bylaws to see that it solves the assembly's problems without creating any new ones. There is no shame in revising a draft a dozen times. Ernest Hemingway rewrote the ending of *Farewell to Arms* thirty-nine times before he was satisfied. When an interviewer asked what the problem was, Hemingway replied, "Getting the words right." Bylaws are important documents. When drafting or amending the basic governing document of your assembly, it is worth the time and effort to get the words right. Remember, good bylaws are not written; they are re-written.

Step Six: The Committee Chairman Reports to the Assembly.

When the committee has approved the draft of the bylaws, the chairman presents the committee's report to a meeting of the assembly. If the committee is presenting a revision of bylaws, the committee and the presiding officer of the assembly should insure that any requirements for previous notice have been met. It is good practice to give every member of an organization a written copy of amendments to or revisions of the bylaws before the meeting at which they will be considered.

When the time for the committee's report arrives, the chairman of the committee proceeds as follows:

COMMITTEE "Mr. Chairman, the committee ap-
CHAIR: pointed to draw up [or "revise"] the by-
                laws has agreed upon the following
                draft [or "revision"] and has directed
                me to move its adoption."

The chairman of the committee then reads the proposed bylaws. If the bylaws are short and uncomplicated and if members have had the opportunity to study them before the meeting, the chair may ask unanimous consent that the first reading of the bylaws may be omitted. In most cases, however, they should be read. When the committee chairman has completed reading the bylaws, he moves their adoption:

COMMITTEE "Mr. Chairman, on behalf of the com-
CHAIR: mittee, I move the adoption of the by-
                laws."

As with other motions offered by committees, the committee on bylaws' motion to adopt the bylaws does not require a second. If the bylaws are short, simple, and few or no amendments are expected, the chair may state the question on their adoption as follows:

CHAIR: The question is on the adoption of the bylaws
           as proposed by the committee. The bylaws

are now open to amendment. Are there any amendments?

Step Seven: The Assembly Considers the Committee's Report and Adopts the Bylaws.

The motion to adopt bylaws is a main motion. As with other main motions, once the chair states the question on the motion, the assembly is free to debate the question, amend the proposed bylaws, postpone their consideration, or recommit them to the committee for further study or revision. If amendments are offered from the floor, they are considered and voted upon one at a time, following the regular rules governing the motion to amend. Though adoption of a revision of or an amendment to bylaws usually requires more than a majority vote, amending the revision or the amendment itself requires only a majority vote.

If the proposed bylaws are long, complex, or contain controversial points, they should be considered seriatim, that is paragraph by paragraph. In such cases, the chair directs the chairman of the committee or the secretary to read each article or paragraph, one at a time. After each article or paragraph is read, the chair announces that it is open to debate and amendment. When amendment of and debate on that article are complete, the next article is read and considered. No article should be adopted until every part of the bylaws has been opened to amendment. The committee chairman should carefully explain each section. When bylaws are considered seriatim, the chair states the question on their adoption this way:

CHAIR: The question is on the adoption of the bylaws as proposed by the committee. The committee chairman will now read the proposed bylaws one paragraph at a time. After each paragraph is read, it will be open for debate and amendment. No paragraph or article will be adopted until all articles have been opened to amendment.

When the last paragraph has been considered, the chair gives the assembly one final chance to offer additional amendments to any article in the bylaws:

CHAIR: The entire set of bylaws is now open to amendment. Are there any further amendments?

If new amendments are proposed during consideration of the bylaws, the assembly may choose to vote to recommit the bylaws to the committee for further study and recommendation, with instructions to report at a later meeting. It is also in order to postpone consideration of the bylaws to a later meeting so that members may weigh amendments or discussion arising out of the initial consideration of the bylaws. When there are no further amendments, the chair puts the question on adopting the bylaws:

CHAIR: The question is on the adoption of the bylaws as proposed by the committee [or "as amended"]. As many as are in favor of adopting the bylaws, say 'aye.' Those opposed, say 'no.' The ayes have it and the bylaws are adopted.

An initial set of bylaws for a new church or organization is adopted by a simple majority vote. A revision of an organization's bylaws is adopted by whatever vote is required to amend those bylaws, usually two-thirds. Once bylaws are adopted, they immediately take effect, unless the motion to adopt the bylaws contains a proviso that specifies otherwise.

The final vote to adopt or amend bylaws should be counted and the results recorded in the minutes.

Content of Bylaws

Though the actual number and content of bylaws will depend upon the size and nature of each assembly, the following bylaws articles are typical:

Article I. Name

This article sets forth the official name of the organization. If incorporated, the corporate charter will state the organization's name and this article may be omitted from the bylaws.

Article II. Mission (Purpose or Object)

The mission article states the purpose or purposes for which your assembly was formed.[3] The mission article should be no longer than one paragraph. It may even be a single sentence, with the various aspects of the assembly's purpose written in parallel phrases set off by semicolons. It should be general enough to completely encompass the assembly's aims, since a two-thirds vote is required for an assembly to consider business that is outside the statement of purpose in its bylaws or charter. If your assembly is incorporated, the statement of purpose should be in the corporate charter and may be omitted from the bylaws.

The mission article is the most important in the entire document. It defines an assembly's underlying reason for being and its fundamental sense of direction. The mission statement should say in a clear, compelling fashion why this particular church or organization exists, for whose benefit, and what it is trying to accomplish. For example, the mission statement of one new inner-city congregation looks like this:

Article II.

Mission

The mission of the Fern Banks Church is to develop a strong, growing fellowship of believers in the Fern Banks community who celebrate God's presence, communicate God's Word, educate God's people, and demonstrate God's love. Our aim is to serve the needs of the people of our community through a New Testament church characterized by uncomplicated and inspiring worship, a Bible-centered, life-related message, and genuine friendship and caring.

Article III. Members

The bylaws should state who is eligible for membership in the assembly, how a person becomes a member, and any special requirements, duties, or privileges of membership. Draft this section with care because rules protecting the basic rights of members cannot be suspended, even by a unanimous vote.

Article IV. Officers

Separate sections of this article should name all officers by their proper titles and describe their duties, qualifications, method of nomination and election, and terms of office.

For many assemblies the duties of officers may be simply described by this standard provision:

These officers shall perform the duties prescribed by these bylaws and the parliamentary authority adopted by the assembly.

If your assembly requires special duties of its officers, define these duties in the article on officers. Be careful, however that no specific duty expected of your officers is omitted. Any mention of specific duties carries with it the implication that duties not specified are not required. If your bylaws have a section defining specific duties of officers, that section should end with this provision:

> . . . and such other duties applicable to the office as prescribed by the parliamentary authority adopted by the assembly.

Your bylaws should say whether officers are nominated from the floor, by a committee, by mail, by petition, or by some other method. If no method of nominating officers is specified in the bylaws, nominations are made from the floor. One of the other methods of nominating candidates may be used in a given election, provided that at the time of the election the assembly adopts a motion specifying the method. A motion prescribing the method of nominating candidates is an incidental motion adopted by a majority vote.

Your bylaws should also specify the method by which officers are elected. As with nominations, if no method is prescribed by the bylaws, any member may make a motion to determine the procedure for the election. The best method of electing officers is by ballot. Barring special circumstances or precedent within your assembly, your bylaws should specify that officers be elected by ballot. If the assembly desires to elect officers by plurality vote, preferential voting, voting by mail, or some other method, the bylaws should specific the method to be used.

Bylaws should also define the terms of office for all officers. The recommended wording is:

> The officers shall be elected by ballot to serve for a term of _____ year(s) or until their successors are

elected, and their terms of office shall begin at the close of the annual meeting at which they are elected.

Avoid setting an unqualified term for any office, such as "for a term of two years." The unqualified wording has two disadvantages. First, it means that on the day the term ends the assembly would be without officers if no new ones have been elected. Second, the assembly is restricted in its method of dealing with an officer guilty of misconduct or neglect of duty in office. Under the wording "for a term of _____ years or until their successors are elected," an assembly can rescind the election of an officer and elect a successor to fill the remainder of the term. Unless the assembly has a prescribed method of disciplining officers, if the unqualified wording "for a term of _____ years" is used, an officer may be removed from office only by a formal trial as described in *Robert's Rules of Order Newly Revised* under "Disciplinary Procedures."

Article V. Meetings

Meetings are the basic events of deliberative assemblies. The bylaws should fix the time and place of regular meetings, state how and by whom special meetings may be called, make provisions for an annual meeting, and establish a quorum for all meetings.

If flexibility in setting dates for regular meetings is desired, the section on regular meetings should be worded like this:

> Section _____. Regular meetings of the congregation shall be held on the first Sunday of January, April, July, and September unless otherwise ordered by the congregation or by the board.

The article on meetings should contain a separate section providing for an annual meeting, such as this:

Section _____. The regular meeting on the second Tuesday in September is the annual meeting and is for the purpose of electing officers, receiving reports of officers and committees, and for any other business that may arise.

Another section should provide for the calling of special meetings to handle urgent business that cannot wait until the next regular meeting of the assembly. For example:

Section _____. Special meetings shall be called by the Chairman of the Board of Elders upon the written request of twenty-five members of the congregation. The date, time, place, and purpose of the meeting shall be stated in the call. At least two weeks notice of the meeting shall be given by printing the call of the meeting in the church newsletter or by reading it during the Sunday morning worship service.

Another section should establish how many members constitute a quorum. Some assemblies use a percentage, but the preferred method is to use a number, which avoids re-computing the quorum each time there is a change in membership. A quorum should not be so low that it allows an unrepresentatively small minority to make decisions for the entire assembly, nor so high that you are unable to hold meetings because you can't get a quorum. A good place to set the quorum is just below the number of members who usually attend your meetings.

Article VI. Board of Directors (Elders, Deacons, Trustees, etc.)

If the assembly has a governing board, then its composition, duties, and powers should be carefully defined by the bylaws. The section on "Boards" in chapter 6 should be helpful to you here.

Article VII. Committees

The bylaws should also define the composition, duties, and powers of each standing committee. See the section on "Standing Committees" in chapter 6.

Article VIII. Parliamentary Authority

Most assemblies adopt a standard manual of parliamentary procedure as their parliamentary authority. This article can be a single sentence that says:

> The rules contained in the current edition of *Robert's Rules of Order Newly Revised* govern this assembly in all cases to which they are applicable and in which they are not inconsistent with these bylaws and any special rules of order the assembly may adopt.

Article IX. Amendment of Bylaws

Don't forget this last article. Bylaws should always provide for their own amendment. A standard wording for this article is: "These bylaws may be amended at any regular meeting of the assembly by a two-thirds vote, provided that the amendment has been submitted in writing at the previous regular meeting."

Amending Bylaws

Once your assembly's bylaws are in place, they may be amended by the motion to *Amend Something Previously Adopted*. The rules governing this motion are the same as those governing main motions with a few additional requirements.

One of those requirements is that amendment of bylaws usually requires previous notice and a two-thirds vote. Amendments to your bylaws should meet whatever requirement the bylaws set for their own amendment.

Another requirement is that any amendment of the by-laws must be within the scope of the notice to amend the bylaws. For example, suppose that during a meeting, a member gave the following notice:

> MEMBER: I give notice that at the next regular meeting I will move to amend Article III, Section 3 of the bylaws to strike the word eighteen and insert the word twenty-one, so that if amended, the section would read: "Only those members who have reached the age of twenty-one years may participate in business meetings or hold office in the church."

Under such a notice, the assembly could adopt any bylaws amendment that would set the age requirement anywhere between the current provision of eighteen and the proposed provision of twenty-one. The assembly could not, however, exceed the extent of the notice, for example, making the required age twenty-two or seventeen. The reason for this rule is to protect absent members from being taken advantage of by members who might propose a minor change in their notice, then propose an extensive change when the amendment comes before the assembly for consideration.

If a proposed amendment to the bylaws is lengthy or involves more than one section of the document, it should be considered paragraph by paragraph.

A bylaws amendment goes into effect immediately unless the motion to adopt the amendment specifies some later time. Such a specification is called a *proviso*. For example, the following clause could appear at the end of a bylaws amendment:

. . . provided, however, that this amendment does not go into effect until after the close of the annual meeting at which it is adopted.

Tips on Drafting Bylaws and Amendments to Bylaws

1. Be Clear.

The first and overriding rule in constructing bylaws is that they be clear. They must say exactly what the assembly wishes them to say, say it all, and say no more. Throughout the drafting process, the bylaws committee should examine their work from the perspective of the officers and members who will use the bylaws after they are adopted. Even the slightest room for confusion can have adverse effects on the assembly's ability to conduct its business.

In 1985, Bylaw 16 of the Southern Baptist Convention contained the following provision for the selection of the convention's Committee on Boards, Commissions, and Standing Committees:

> The Committee on Boards, Commissions, and Standing Committees shall be composed of two (2) members from each qualified state, who shall be nominated to the convention by the Committee on Committees.

During the 1985 session of the SBC, a messenger attempted to nominate other candidates from the floor by moving a substitute amendment to the Committee on Committees' report. The chair first ruled that nominations from the floor would be allowed, but that they must be made state by state. Following an appeal of the chair's ruling and a recess, the chair later ruled, on the advice of the parliamentarians, that nominations from the floor were out of order. The convention elected the original slate of nominees offered by the Committee on Committees, but confusion over the bylaw led messengers who wanted to nominate candidates from the floor to believe they had been denied a right to which they were entitled.

Though, according to *Robert's Rules of Order Newly Revised*, the usual procedure for nominations by a committee includes the call for further nominations from the floor, in the case of nominations for the Committee on Boards, Commissions, and Standing Committees, Bylaw 16 said the committee "shall be composed of . . . members . . . who shall be nominated to the Convention by the Committee on Committees." Thus, in addition to establishing the duty of the Committee on Committees to nominate members of the Committee on Boards, Commissions, and Standing Committees, Bylaw 16 also appeared to establish an *eligibility requirement* for members of the Committee on Boards, Commissions, and Standing Committees, namely that they be nominees of the Committee on Committees. Under this interpretation, nominations from the floor for the Committee on Boards, Commissions, and Standing Committees were out of order.

Disagreement over the chair's ruling on this bylaw resulted in a group of messengers suing the convention. Though the suit was eventually dismissed by a state appellate court and rejected by the United States Supreme Court, the two-year legal conflict cost the convention over a quarter of a million dollars.

In an effort to resolve confusion and to clearly permit messengers to nominate candidates for the Committee on Boards, Commissions, and Standing Committees from the floor, the convention's Executive Committee recommended that Bylaw 16 be amended to read:

The Committee on Boards, Commissions, and Standing Committees shall be composed of two (2) members from each qualified state, who shall be elected by the convention. Nominations for each position shall be made by the Committee on Committees. Further nominations may be made from the floor. No messenger shall be allowed to nominate more than one person at one time for election to the Committee on Boards, Commissions, and Standing Committees.

During the 1986 annual session, the convention adopted the amendment to Bylaw 16 and has operated smoothly under the amended bylaw for the past four years.

The point of this story is that bylaws must be clear. They must be written in such a way that they say exactly what they mean, and mean exactly what they say. Write as tightly as possible. Pay careful attention to punctuation. Attempt to construct each sentence so that it is impossible to misunderstand or to quote out of context. Be clear.

2. Keep the Bylaws as Simple as Possible.

As with all parliamentary rules, the purpose of bylaws is to facilitate the fair, orderly, and efficient transaction of business by organizations. A cumbersome, overly restrictive set of bylaws will stifle an assembly and frustrate members who want to get things done. Hence, bylaws should be no more detailed or restrictive than necessary.

Ultimately, the success of an organization rests upon the wisdom and judgment exercised by its members and leaders. No set of bylaws can be comprehensive enough to prevent every mistake an assembly is likely to make or to compel the proper action in every circumstance. If your bylaws accurately define the basic operating structure of your assembly, the basic rights and obligations of its members, and the fundamental principles by which you wish to conduct your business, they have done enough. Bylaws should guide an assembly, not choke it. Keep them simple.

3. Be Consistent.

Though variety of expression is a desirable stylistic quality for an essay or a speech, it can be disastrous in a set of bylaws. Be consistent. Use the same word or phrase to denote the same thing throughout the document. Use different words to denote different things. Do not use synonyms.

For example, if you use the word *church* to denote your entire assembly as a corporate entity including members, officers, and committees, do not use the word *church* again to denote something else, such as a congregational meeting. Use another term such as "the congregation."

Consistency should also extend to the arrangement of similar paragraphs or sections. If two paragraphs are similar in substance, give them a similar arrangement. For example, an article defining the membership, election, duties, and so forth of standing committees should be composed of parallel sections:

> Section 3. A Finance Committee composed of the treasurer and four deacons shall be elected by the congregation at the annual meeting. The committee shall . . . .
> Section 4. A Youth Committee composed of five members shall be appointed by the Youth Minister promptly after the annual meeting. The committee shall . . . .

Consistency and parallel arrangement in drafting bylaws will help both drafters and members to recognize and compare similar provisions within the bylaws. Recognition and comparison are important to drafters because they improve the accuracy of the draft, and they are important to members because they make the resulting by-laws easier to use.

4. Use the Present Tense and the Indicative Mood.

Rules of all kinds, including bylaws, should be written to speak as of the time they are being applied, not as of the time they are written or adopted. Hence, you should use the present tense when drafting bylaws.

To avoid ambiguity or confusion, the words *shall* and *may not* should be used only to convey that to accomplish something, someone must act or refrain from acting. If you wish to declare a rule of conduct, use "shall." If you wish to declare a result, don't. Use the indicative rather than the imperative mood to make declarative statements. For example, do not say, "Any baptized believer shall be eligible for membership in the church." Say, "Any baptized believer is eligible . . ."

5. Keep Related Items Together.

Place everything relating to a single subject in the same or adjacent articles. Extensive use of cross-referencing makes the document harder to use. Be especially careful to include exceptions within the sentences to which they apply.

Summary

As we noted in the introduction, the best way to avoid a misunderstanding is to have an understanding. A good set of bylaws constitutes an agreement between members of an assembly to conduct their business in a particular way. When officers and members know and conduct themselves according to an agreed upon set of rules, there are fewer opportunities for misunderstanding.

Be familiar with your bylaws. Keep them in working order through amendments or revisions as needed. See that the secretary of your assembly provides every new member receives a copy of the bylaws. And, above all, follow the rules.

Notes

1. From a legal standpoint a church's bylaws or corporate charter are the highest body of rules governing its business. However, as we noted in the first chapter, the Bible stands above whatever man-made rules a religious assembly may choose to help them conduct their business. Bylaws should be viewed as a written understanding of how a given church will apply the principles of Scripture to the administration of its affairs.

2. The American Institute of Parliamentarians publishes an annual directory of professional parliamentarians. A copy of the directory or a list of professional parliamentarians in your area is available from the Executive Director, American Institute of Parliamentarians, 124 West Washington Blvd., P.O. Box 12452, Ft. Wayne IN 46863.

3. *Robert's Rules of Order Newly Revised* and most other parliamentary manuals use the terms "Object" or "Purpose" article. I prefer the term "Mission" because it is more appropriate to describing a church or church-related assembly's reasons for existing, and it suggests that the statement is more than a mere legal description of the organization.

Glossary

Abstain: To refrain from voting. A member has the right to abstain from voting on any issue.

Adjourn: To officially close a meeting. The motion to *Adjourn* is usually a privileged motion.

Adjourned Meeting: The continuation of an earlier regular or special meeting that adjourned before completing its agenda.

Adopt: To approve a motion by whatever vote the motion requires.

Adopt a report: To approve and make every assertion in a report the official statement of the assembly.

The Affirmative: The members voting yes on a rising or a counted vote.

Agenda: The official list of items of business planned for consideration during a meeting or convention.

Amend: The subsidiary motion to change the wording of another motion.

Amend Something Previously Adopted: The restorative motion to change the wording of a motion adopted at a previous meeting.

Announcing the Result of a Vote: The formal announcement by the chair that a motion was carried or lost.

Annual Meeting: A yearly meeting to elect officers and to hear annual reports of officers and committees.

Appeal: The incidental motion to allow the assembly to sustain or overrule a ruling of the chair.

Approval of Minutes: The formal acceptance by the assembly of the secretary's minutes of a meeting, which makes those minutes the official record of the assembly's proceedings.

Articles of Incorporation: See **Corporate Charter.**

Ayes: The members voting yes on a voice vote.

Ballot Vote: Any method of voting that allows the voter to secretly express his choice. Ballot votes are usually cast by marking a piece of paper or voting by a machine.

Board: A special kind of committee, usually composed of the officers of an assembly and other directors, that governs an assembly or supervises its affairs between meetings of the general membership.

Bylaws: The basic, self-imposed rules of an assembly that define its purpose, structure and internal government. See also *Corporate Charter*.

Calling a Member to Order: An order from the chairman for a member to be seated because he is disorderly or has violated a rule relating to decorum in debate.

Call for the Orders of the Day: The privileged motion that requires the chairman to enforce the agenda when he has failed to do so. The motion is a demand that may be made by a single member and does not require a vote.

Call to Order: The official declaration by the chair that the meeting has begun.

Call of the Meeting: The official notice of a special meeting given to every member of an assembly.

Called Meeting: A *special meeting*.

Chair: The chairman or presiding officer of a deliberative assembly.

Commit: Another name for the motion to *Refer to Committee*.

Committee: A group of members to whom an assembly has committed some specialized task. Committees are usually created to study or investigate an issue, to recommend action, or to act on behalf of the assembly in a certain matter.

Consider: To discuss and decide upon a pending motion.

Convention: An assembly of delegates who represent constituent units of an organization and act in the name of the entire group.

Corporate Charter: A legal document, granted by the state, that defines the purpose and structure of an incorporated body. Whereas bylaws are an agreement between members of an organization, a corporate charter is an agreement between an organization and the government that issues the charter.

Credentials Committee: The convention committee that registers delegates, verifies their credentials, and presents to the convention a list of registered delegates.

Debate: The formal discussion of a motion by members in a meeting.

Debatable: Motions that may be debated are said to be *debatable*.

Delegate: A voting member of a convention.

Deliberative Assembly: A group of people meeting to discuss and collectively decide upon action to be taken in the name of the entire group.

Demand: Any call for a parliamentary action that a member has the right to assert by himself.

Dilatory Tactics: Any misuse of procedure aimed at obstructing business.

Discharge a Committee: The restorative motion that takes from a committee a matter previously referred to it.

Dispense with Reading of Minutes: To postpone the reading and approval of minutes.

Dispose of: To remove a motion from consideration by voting to adopt, reject, postpone, refer, or table the motion.

Division of a Question: The incidental motion to divide a pending question that is composed of several independent parts so that the parts may be considered and voted upon separately.

Division of the Assembly: The incidental motion to require the chairman to take a rising vote when a voice vote is inconclusive. The motion is a demand that may be made by a single member and does not require a vote.

Ex-officio Member: A member who serves on a committee or a board by virtue of holding some other office or position.

Executive Session: Any meeting or part of a meeting that is held in secret.

Fix the Time to Which to Adjourn: The privileged motion to set a time for another meeting to continue the business of the present session.

Floor: A member is "assigned the floor" when the chair recognizes him. As long as he "has the floor" he is the only member entitled to make a motion or to speak. when he has finished speaking or his time to speak has expired, the member is said to "yield the floor."

General Consent: An informal method of voting by assuming unanimous approval of a motion or an action unless some member objects.

General Order: A motion that is scheduled to be considered at a certain meeting without a specific time being set for its consideration.

Immediately Pending Question: The last motion stated by the chair and, therefore, open for consideration by the assembly.

Incidental Main Motion: A subsidiary, privileged, or incidental motion that is made while no other business is pending and is, therefore, treated as a main motion.

Incidental Motions: The class of motions that take care of procedural matters that arise while handling business in a meeting.

In Order: Any action that, at a particular time, can be done under the rules is said to be *in order*.

Lay on the Table: The subsidiary motion that temporarily sets aside pending business so that a more urgent matter can be considered immediately.

Limit or Extend Debate: The subsidiary motion that sets or extends a previously set time limit for discussion of a pending question or of debate in general.

Main Motion: The class of motions that introduce subjects in a meeting.

Majority Vote: More than half of the legal votes cast for a motion or a candidate.

Make a Motion: To formally propose a motion for the assembly's consideration and decision.

Meeting: An official gathering of the members of a deliberative assembly to conduct business.

Minority Report: A report by members of a committee who wish to formally express their dissent from the committee's report.

Minutes: The official record of an assembly's proceedings.

Motion: A formal proposal made by a member in a meeting that the assembly say or do something.

New Business: Any new item of business to be considered in a meeting.

The Negative: The members voting no on a rising or a counted vote.

Noes: The members voting no on a voice vote.

Notice: See *Previous Notice.*

Objection: The formal expression of opposition by a member to a proposed action.

Old Business: See *Unfinished Business.*

Order of Business: The adopted order in which various classes of business will be taken up in a meeting.

Orders of the Day: Items of business that have been previously scheduled to be taken up at a certain meeting or time.

Out of Order: Any action that would violate an assembly's rules is said to be *out of order.*

Parliamentarian: An expert in parliamentary procedure whose duty is to advise the chair on procedural matters in a meeting.

Parliamentary Authority: The parliamentary manual adopted by an assembly as its parliamentary guide and general roles of order.

Parliamentary Inquiry: The incidental motion used by a member to direct a procedural question to the presiding officer.

Parliamentary Procedure: The rules and customs that govern deliberative assemblies.

Pending: A motion is said to be *pending* from the time it is stated by the chair until it has been disposed of.

Point of Information: The incidental motion used by a member to direct a factual question to the presiding officer or through him to another member.

Point of Order: The incidental motion that calls the chairman's attention to a breech of the rules.

Postpone Indefinitely: The subsidiary motion that suppresses or kills a main motion without permitting it to come to a direct vote.

Postpone to a Certain Time: The subsidiary motion that delays consideration of a pending question until a certain time or until after a certain event.

Precedence: A motion's parliamentary rank, which determines when it can be introduced, considered, and put to a vote.

Previous Notice: The formal notification of members that a meeting will be held or that a certain action will be proposed at a meeting.

Previous Question: The subsidiary motion that closes debate and brings a pending question to a vote.

Privileged Motions: The class of motions that have nothing to do with pending questions, but with certain matters of overriding importance. The privileged motions are: *Call for the Orders of the Day, Question of Privilege, Recess, Adjourn,* and *Fix the Time to Which to Adjourn.*

Procedural Motions: Motions that deal with questions of procedure rather than substantive proposals as do main motions.

Program Committee: The convention committee that plans and proposes a complete order of business for the convention.

Putting the Question: The chair *puts the question* on a motion when he takes a vote on it.

Question: Any motion or proposal submitted to an assembly for their decision. The immediately pending motion is usually referred to as *the question.*

Question of Privilege: The privileged motion that permits an assembly to interrupt pending business to consider some urgent matter that relates to the comfort, safety, or integrity of the assembly or of an individual member.

Quorum: The number or percentage of members that must be present in order to legally conduct business in a meeting.

Rank: A motion's position in the order of precedence.

Reading and Approval of Minutes: See *Approval of Minutes.*

Receive a Report: To formally allow a committee or an officer to present a report.

Recess: The privileged motion to take a short intermission in a meeting without adjourning the meeting.

Recognition: The formal assignment of the floor by the chair to a member who wishes to speak or to make a motion.

Recommendation: A motion made by an officer or a committee during a report to the assembly.

Reconsider: The restorative motion to bring back for further consideration a motion that was voted on earlier in the meeting.

Reconsider and Enter on the Minutes: A special form of the motion to *Reconsider* that allows two members to suspend action on a main motion until the next meeting.

Refer to Committee: The subsidiary motion to send a pending motion to a committee for further study or action.

Regular Meeting: The stated periodic business sessions of a permanent organization.

Repeal: See *Rescind.*

Report: An official statement of an officer or a committee concerning some matter the assembly has assigned to that officer or committee.

Rescind: The restorative motion to undo an action taken at a previous meeting.

Resolution: A motion, introduced by the word *Resolved,* that formally states the assembly's position on an issue.

Restorative Motions: The class of motions that bring back for further consideration some matter that was before the assembly but has already been disposed of.

Rising Vote: A vote taken by asking the affirmative, then the negative to stand, with the chair judging which side is in the majority.

Rules of Order: The rules of an assembly that relate to procedural matters in meetings.

Rules Committee: The convention committee that drafts and presents a set of standing rules for the convention.

Ruling: Any stated decision of the presiding officer that relates to procedural matters in a meeting.

Second: To formally indicate one's willingness to consider a motion just made by another member.

Secretary: The officer of a deliberative assembly who records the assembly's proceedings.

Session: A meeting or series of meetings that conducts a single agenda. If an assembly requires several meetings to complete an agenda, such as in a convention, each separate gathering is called a *meeting* and the series of meetings is called a *session.*

Show of Hands: A vote taken by asking the affirmative, then the negative to raise their hands, with the chair judging which side is in the majority.

Special Committee: Any temporary committee created to perform some special task and which ceases to exist when that task is completed.

Special Meeting: A meeting called to handle urgent business that cannot wait until the next *regular meeting.*

Special Order: A motion postponed by a two-thirds vote that is allowed to interrupt whatever business pending when the time for its consideration arrives.

Standing Committee: Any permanent committee, usually established by the bylaws, that performs some continuing function.

Standing Rules: The rules of an assembly that relate to general administrative policies.

Stating the Question: The formal statement of a motion to the assembly by the chair after it has been moved and seconded.

Subsidiary Motions: The class of motions that assist an assembly in disposing of main motions. The subsidiary motions are: *Postpone Indefinitely, Amend, Refer to Committee, Postpone to a Certain Time, Limit or Extend Debate, Previous Question,* and *Lay on the Table.*

Substitute: To amend a motion by proposing to replace it with a new motion on the same subject.

Suspend the Rules: The incidental motion to take an action that would ordinarily violate the assembly's rules of procedure.

Table: See *Lay on the Table.*

Take From the Table: The restorative motion to bring back for further consideration a motion previously laid on the table.

Teller: A member appointed by the chair to assist him in counting votes.

Tie Vote: A vote that is equally divided between the affirmative and the negative. A tie vote is not a deadlock but has the same effect as a negative vote.

Two-thirds Vote: At least two-thirds of the legal votes cast. In a two-thirds vote the number of affirmative votes is at least double that of the negative votes.

Unanimous Consent: See *General Consent.*

Unfinished Business: Any item of business left over from a previous meeting that adjourned before completing its agenda.

Voice Vote: A vote taken by asking all in favor of a motion to say aye, then those opposed to say no, with the chair judging as to which side is in the majority by the volume of each response.